KU-425-825

MONSTERS & MYSTERIOUS PLACES

BLITZ EDITIONS

Copyright © Bookmart Ltd/Amazon Publishing Ltd 1993

All rights reserved. No part of this publication may be reproduced,
stored in a retrieval system, or transmitted in any form or by any
means, electronic, mechanical, photocopying, recording or otherwise,
without prior written permission from the publishers.

Published by Blitz Editions
an imprint of Bookmart Ltd
Registered Number 2372865
Trading as Bookmart Ltd, Desford Road, Enderby
Leicester LE9 5AD

Cover design: Peter Dolton
Text design: Jim Reader
Production Manager: Sue Gray
Editorial Manager: Roz Williams

Printed in the Slovak Republic
50976

ISBN 1 85605 131 5

Every effort has been made to contact the copyright holders for the pictures.
In some cases they have been untraceable, for which we offer our apologies.
Thanks to the Fortean Picture Library and the Hulton Deutsch Collection Ltd, who supplied them.
The Hulton Deutsch Collection Ltd have provided the following: pp 2, 3, 9 bottom, 10, 18, 26, 27, 28 bottom,
29, 30, 33, 40 top left, 41 bottom, 42, 51, 52 bottom, 53 bottom, 54 top, 60–4, 75 top, 76 top, 79.
The remainder have been supplied by the Fortean Picture Library.
Cover: The Hulton Deutsch Collection Ltd supplied the picture on the back.
Those on the front were supplied by the Fortean Picture Library.

The Author
Reuben Stone has long been fascinated by the paranormal
and the mysteries of the unexplained. He is the author of many books
and articles on military history, popular science and technology,
and various aspects of anomalous phenomena.

MONSTERS & MYSTERIOUS PLACES

WHAT LURKS IN THE LAKE?

For over 1000 years there have been authenticated sightings of a monstrous creature living in one of the Earth's deepest lakes. Now scientists have finally begun to take the stories seriously, and are using state-of-the-art technology to get to the bottom of the icy black waters of Loch Ness and the secrets they hide...

There can hardly be a person in the civilized world who has not heard of Loch Ness in Scotland and its famous monster. Possibly rather less commonly known is the fact that Nessie is but one of an army of such unexplained lake monsters. There are about 250 lakes, world-wide, which reputedly harbour creatures that, according to conventional science, should not be there – or anywhere – at all.

The first intimation that something strange might be living in Loch Ness came in St Adamnan's 7th-century biography of St Columba. In about 565 AD the latter apparently confronted a water monster living in the River Ness with the sign of the cross and so, according to Adamnan, caused it to depart the neighbourhood at speed. Over the centuries other sightings were made, although some have the curious feature that the creature was seen on land, not swimming in the Loch itself.

In 1771, for instance, one Patrick Rose saw what he described as a cross between a horse and a camel in the Loch. In 1907 (or 1919, according to some accounts) a group of local children at Invermoriston, which is about five miles from the southern end of the Loch on its western side, saw a 'light brown, camel-like quadruped' slip into the murky depths of this strange stretch of water.

A GAPING RED MOUTH

A curious event occurred in 1857 at Loch Arkaig, which is some 20 miles south-west of Loch Ness but linked to it by the same river system, so there may well be a connection of another kind with the creature reportedly living in Loch Ness.

Lord Malmesbury, a solid, bewhiskered gentleman rolled from the stoutest Victorian makings, went shooting deer near Loch Arkaig that autumn. His memoir of 3 October 1857 reads:

'This morning my stalker and his boy gave me an account of a mysterious creature, which they say exists in Loch Arkaig, and which they call the Lake Horse. It is the same animal of which one has occasionally read accounts in newspapers as having been seen in the

While St Columba was in the Highlands, preaching to the Picts in the late 6th century (above), he chanced on a monster in the River Ness. The record of his encounter is the first written account of a sighting of the mysterious creature that inhabits the deep, peat-stained waters of brooding Loch Ness (opposite).

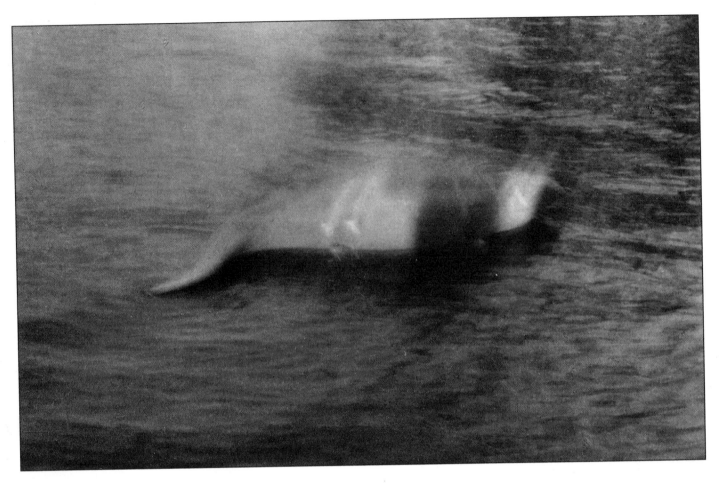

Above: *The first photograph, taken in 1933, that was alleged to show the Loch Ness monster. Sceptics have remarked that it could show a labrador swimming with a stick in its mouth. Despite often unsatisfactory photographic evidence, there seems little doubt that something unusual lives in Loch Ness.*

Highland lochs, and on the existence of which the late Lord Ellesmere wrote an interesting article…

'My stalker, John Stewart, at Achnacarry, has seen it twice, and both times at sunrise in summer on a bright sunny day, when there was not a ripple on the water. The creature was basking on the surface; he only saw the head and the hindquarters, proving that its back was hollow, which is not the shape of any fish or of a seal. Its head resembled that of a horse.'

Local folk, then, were not unfamiliar with the presence of odd animals in the inland waters of the Highlands. Most witnesses described something with two humps, a tail, and a snake-like head. They often noted a V-shaped wash behind the creature, and commonly reported such details as a gaping red mouth and horns or antennae on the top of its head.

Children of the villages around Loch Ness were told not to go swimming in its waters lest the creatures that lived there attack them, but word of what might be in Loch Ness did not travel far. The bombshell, as far as the world outside was concerned, came in 1933. Up to a point,

this has a simple, material explanation. In that year a road was dynamited into existence along the Loch's north shore, and the view across the water 'improved' by sawing away the vegetation. Tourism into the area immediately increased. So did sightings of the thing in the lake, but now they were not being made simply by local people.

'PREHISTORIC ANIMAL'

On 14 April 1933, a Mr and Mrs Mackay catapulted the Loch Ness monster into the headlines. The Inverness *Courier* reported their account of seeing an unknown creature in the Loch that 'disported itself for fully a minute, its body resembling that of a whale'. More sightings, and photographs to prove them, followed rapidly.

At 4 pm on 22 July 1933, Londoners Mr and Mrs George Spicer were driving along beside Loch Ness on the new road, on their way back from a holiday in northern Scotland, when their car nearly struck a huge, black creature with a long neck. The 'prehistoric animal', as Mr Spicer described it, shambled across the road, slithered through the undergrowth, and splashed into the Loch.

On 12 November 1933, an employee of the British Aluminium Company, Hugh Gray, watched an unusually large 'object' rise out of the Loch. When it had raised itself two or three feet out of the water, Gray photographed it. He estimated the length of the thing to be about 40 ft, and described it as having greyish-coloured, smooth and shiny skin.

His photograph is, to say the least, ambiguous: it's not difficult to see in it the image of a labrador-like dog with a largish piece of wood in its mouth. But in late 1933, a little frivolity from the Highlands was good news to a world wearied by the Depression and worried by Hitler's recent rise to power. The picture was published in papers all over the globe, and the Loch Ness monster became a permanent fixture in the popular imagination. In the year after the release of the Gray photograph, there were over 50 reported sightings of 'Nessie'.

In 1934 two more photographs were taken of the creature. One was by Colonel Robert Wilson, a London doctor. Labelled the 'surgeon's picture' by the British press, Wilson's photo was clear and distinct in comparison with Gray's. It seemed to show the head and neck of a plesiosaur-like creature rising out of the water. In the summer of that year, Sir Edward Mountain organized an expedition to the Loch to investigate the stories and the sightings. A member of the group snapped a picture of something strange breaking the surface of the Loch on 13 July, but hardly any details are visible.

POMPOUS JOKE?

Since then, there have been many pictures taken of things that may or may not be mysterious animals in Loch Ness. Several have been definite hoaxes. One – taken by a notorious self-publicizing 'investigator' – was nothing more than a part-submerged fence post with a sock, or possibly a collapsed Wellington boot, stuck on top to look like the head of a monster. This kind of joke hardly forwards the cause of disinterested research.

Others, even some of those taken by

Above: *The 'surgeon's picture' of Nessie, taken on 19 April 1934 by London doctor Colonel Robert Wilson, showing the classic plesiosaur-like profile of the mystery animal.*

reputable and impartial scientists, have been ambiguous at best, although not necessarily because of what they seem to show. The classic examples are the underwater pictures taken by Dr Robert H. Rines of the Academy of Applied Sciences at the renowned Massachusetts Institute of Technology during thorough surveys of the Loch in 1972 and 1975. One of the computer-enhanced photographs, taken in 1975, seems to show an animal that fits the standard description of Nessie – something rather like an aquatic dinosaur. The other, taken in 1972, apparently shows the creature's flipper.

The doubt arises not just because there is, inevitably, no background or other detail by which to judge the size of the image – Loch Ness's waters are extremely murky thanks to the amount of peat suspended in them – but because of the pompous scientific name dreamed up for the purported animal by the naturalist Sir Peter Scott. Impressed by the rhomboid shape of the flipper, Scott coined the Latin name *Nessiteras rhombopteryx* for the animal, a 'christening' that was taken at the time to be a sign that Nessie had been accepted into the hallowed groves of establishment science.

Then someone – who must have been either a genius with dyslexia or a fanatical crossword buff – realized that the letters of

---

THEY WATCHED, PETRIFIED WITH FEAR, AS THE PREHISTORIC CREATURE SHAMBLED ACROSS THE ROAD, SLITHERED THROUGH THE UNDERGROWTH, AND SPLASHED INTO THE LOCH.

Below: *Nessie as pictured by Cornish magician and monster-hunter Anthony 'Doc' Shiels on 21 May 1977. Like many other photographs of the creature, its lack of background makes it inconclusive as evidence.*

the Latin name could swiftly be rearranged to read 'Monster hoax by Sir Peter S'. Was it a joke? A revelation? A bizarre coincidence? Scott never said, while sceptics have pointed out that the image in the Rines photographs could have been of nothing more mysterious than a lump of wood.

STRIKING CONSISTENCY

If the photographic evidence is largely dubious, the circumstantial evidence that some very odd animal is alive and well and living in Loch Ness is very good. In the 60 years since 1933, there have been more than 3000 sightings of the creature. There is, to begin with, a striking consistency in reports of what people see. Most describe a long-necked, humpbacked animal that can move very fast when it wants to, whether its head is up or down, and that, at other times, will simply rise quietly to the surface for a few minutes and then sink silently below.

It is also a curious fact that apart from Loch Ness itself the world-wide sightings of lake monsters that resemble Nessie (which no living animal known to science does) have all occurred around the isothermic line of 50°F in both northern and southern hemispheres. The animal, or animals, whatever they are, thus conform to a rule of zoology in having a distinct distribution within a specific environmental pattern. They don't pop up just anywhere, and if they did there would be grounds for suspecting that they were more a figment of the imagination (or folklore) than an elusive fact of nature.

Veteran cryptozoologist Bernard Heuvelmans commented crisply: 'One could hardly wish for better circumstantial evidence for their existence.' The unanswered question remains: what might these animals actually be?

INEXHAUSTIBLE APPETITE

There are numerous theories as to the animal's identity. Candidates have included the zeuglodon, a prehistoric, snake-like primitive whale, an unknown type of long-necked seal, giant eels, and more prosaically walruses, floating mats of plants, otters, diving birds and even – someone had to say it – mirages.

A favourite contender has always been the plesiosaur, a marine reptile that has officially been extinct for the last 70 million years. The 'extinct' label affixed by science is not necessarily proof that a species has in fact died out, however; it simply represents the current state of accepted knowledge. Until 1938 the coelacanth, a singularly ugly but otherwise inoffensive prehistoric fish, was reckoned extinct because there were no fossils of it less than 70 million years old and no living specimens had been seen; but then coelacanths were found thriving, and no doubt thoroughly indifferent to the opinions of scientists, in the Indian Ocean. So it is possible that a community of plesiosaurs has survived in the same way.

The mystery of the Loch Ness monster is riddled with paradoxes. When Canadian holidaymaker Jennifer Bruce took the picture opposite of the view across Urquhart Bay from near Temple Pier in 1982, she did not notice the monster in the Loch. But thorough research by scientist Dr Robert Rines in the 1970s (above and left), produced photographic evidence that was no less ambiguous.

Above: *A model of Issie, the monster said to inhabit Lake Ikeda in Japan.*

Right: *Pictish carvings show a strange elephant-like creature, which some believe represents a lake monster.*

Below: *A fossil relic of Tullimonstrum gregarium, which has been claimed to be an ancestor of Nessie.*

They would have had to survive in the sea for the major part of that time, but they could have found their way into Loch Ness with little or no difficulty in the last 10,000 years. Then, after the last great Ice Age ended, the glaciers retreated, and the Great Glen fault – which divides the Scottish Highlands, and of which Loch Ness is a part – opened up to the sea. On the other hand, they would have had to have adapted from being geared to a saline marine environment to survival in the fresh water of the Loch in a very short time (in evolutionary terms). But that again is not impossible.

Loch Ness is a fairly sterile place, partly because of its depth (up to an estimated 1000 ft), its darkness, and the lack of nutrients flowing into it. But a plesiosaur could survive there on a healthy diet of fish without disturbing the Loch's basic ecosystem. At least, it could as long as it had an inexhaustible appetite for fresh salmon. This is because the mature salmon that enter the Loch from the sea, by way of the River Ness, simply don't eat, and so don't affect the rest of the food chain in the Loch. Still more convenient, salmon come into the Loch all year round, so there is a reasonably consistent and plentiful supply of food for any predator that might depend on them for survival.

THE LAST DINOSAUR?

What militates against Nessie being a leftover plesiosaur is the rarity with which it seems to appear on the surface, for the creature would have to live in the top 125 ft or so of the Loch's waters, not only because that is where the food (of any kind) is, but also because below that level the temperature drops dramatically – too low for a cold-blooded reptile (even of the 'monster's' reported size) to survive. Even the warmer level of the Loch is at the extreme end of such an animal's range. On top of that, reptiles have lungs, not gills: they need to breathe fresh air. So why aren't the 'reptiles' of Loch Ness seen on the surface more often?

Most reptiles, too, would have to come – and stay – ashore for a brief period at least once every year to lay their eggs. No one has seen that happen yet at Loch Ness. It is, of course, again possible that the creatures move from the Loch out to the ocean for some of the year, perhaps especially in the breeding season. Nevertheless, it's surprising that this hasn't been seen happening on some rocky Scottish shore by someone at some time.

Even the possibility that the creature's elusiveness – not to say virtual invisibility

– is the result of there being only a very small family of monsters in the Loch, is hardly a conclusive argument. To be viable, there would need to be a community of an average of at least three monsters alive at any one time. The Loch's surface area is no more than 45 square miles, that is 15 square miles of surface water for every monster. The surface area of the Mediterranean is some 900,000 square miles, or 20,000 times bigger. The estimated population of the rare and endangered monk seal in the Mediterranean is between 300 and 600 or, at best, one every 1500 square miles – 100 times the area for each Loch Ness monster. Seals are mammals and have to breathe air; they surface to do so. And they are seen every year, at all seasons, and recognized with delight for what they are, by all kinds of people all over that huge inland sea. There is no mystery about the monk seal, although they are far more sparsely distributed over a much vaster area than the extremely mysterious Loch Ness monster would seem to be.

A SWIMMING ELEPHANT?

None of that, however, is a conclusive argument against there being something – or some things – living in the Loch. It may not be a reptile at all. It may be a fish of a

Proboscis — Small horn projection

Eyes

Inner Arms (6)

Outer Arms

Funnel

Probable form of 'Elephant Squid' Cephalopod 'Nessie' Doc Shiels 1984

Above: *In 1984 'Doc' Shiels proposed that Nessie was a gigantic elephant squid.*

Left: *A coelacanth, a fish believed to have been extinct for 70 million years until one was caught in 1938. Could lake monsters too be living examples of reptiles officially deemed to be extinct?*

THE HIDEOUS COELACANTH HAD BEEN OFFICIALLY EXTINCT FOR **70** MILLION YEARS UNTIL IT WAS DISCOVERED TO BE ALIVE — AND STILL SWIMMING — IN **1938.**

Above: *The plesiosaur, which of all known animals most resembles 'typical' lake monsters as seen in Europe and North America.*

THE INTREPID COLONEL TRACKED THE ANIMAL AS IT RETURNED TO ITS LAIR.

---

rather unusual variety. It may be something utterly unexpected. In August (not April!) 1979, two highly qualified academics, Dr Dennis Power and Dr Donald Johnson, suggested in the columns of the august journal *New Scientist* that the creature of Loch Ness might be a swimming elephant. While this may have started as a lighthearted article, a correspondent to *Fortean Times* gleefully pointed out a fine, ironic coincidence with this proposal. Ancient Pictish rock carvings showed (among many recognizable creatures) an animal that scholars had been unable to identify and had called either just 'the Pictish beast' or – here it comes – 'the swimming elephant'.

Certainly one of the odder aspects of the Loch Ness monster is its apparent ability to travel over land. In June 1990, retired Colonel L. McP. Fordyce published an account in *Scots Magazine* of his experience in April 1932 – some 12 months before the event usually credited as the first 'modern' sighting of the denizen of the Loch. He too mentioned the resemblance to an elephant.

Colonel Fordyce and his wife were driving south in their six-cylinder Morris Isis, along the minor road on the south side of the Loch from Foyers to Fort Augustus. At one point the road leaves the shoreline and winds through woodland. Colonel Fordyce wrote:

'Travelling at about 25 mph in this wooded section, we were startled to see an enormous animal coming out of the woods on our left and making its way over the road about 150 yards ahead of us, towards the loch.

'It had the gait of an elephant, but looked like a cross between a very large horse and a camel, with a hump on its back and a small head on a long neck.'

Colonel Fordyce was not a soldier for nothing. He got out of his car and followed the animal on foot 'for a short distance. From the rear it looked grey and shaggy. Its long, thin neck gave it the appearance of an elephant with its trunk raised.'

THE MONSTER BITES BACK

So, the mystery deepens and, in its way, becomes almost as murky as the peat-ridden waters of the Loch itself. But one of the most persuasive arguments that a large, strange animal of some kind is living in (or near) Loch Ness is the variety of different traditions and sightings from other, similar lakes around the world that share certain geographic and topographical features with Loch Ness. For the mystery animals are all reported from lake and river systems that either are connected to the sea or have been in the past, and they all either harbour or once harboured migratory fish. Many of the lakes that fit this pattern are also deep and cold.

One such is Lake Storsjön in central Sweden, which is connected by river systems with the Gulf of Bothnia, a spur of the Baltic Sea. For 350 years or more there have been reports of a monster in the lake, and since 1987 alone the local Society for Investigating the Great Lake has collected over 400 reports of sightings. Few, unfortunately, are consistent, so there is no clear idea of what the creature might really look like. Some witnesses have seen an animal with a large neck that undulates back and forth and looks like a horse's mane. Others described a large worm-like creature with distinct 'ears' on its head. According to reports, the beast's size may vary from 10 to 42 ft in length.

By a brilliant irony, one famous sighting was made by a local fisheries conservation officer, Ragnar Björks. The 73-year-old official was out checking fishing permits among anglers on the lake in the 1970s

Left: *An attempt in 1969 to trap the strange animal that several witnesses have reported seeing in Lough Auna, in Ireland's wild Connemara region.*

THERE ARE STARTLING SIMILARITIES BETWEEN THE LAKES AROUND THE WORLD WHICH ARE REPORTEDLY INHABITED BY MONSTERS.

when he had the fright of his life. A huge tail suddenly broke the calm surface near Björks's 12 ft rowing boat. The creature that owned the tail seemed to be 18 ft long, and was grey-brown on top with a yellow underbelly. Björks struck at it with his oar and hit it on the back. The creature reacted by slapping the water mightily with its tail: Björks and his boat were ignominiously hurled about 10 ft in the air. During his brief flight Björks became a convinced believer in lake monsters.

WREAKING VENGEANCE

Inconsistent reports also come from Ireland, where in Connemara a wilderness of rocks and peat-bog is broken up by a patchwork of loughs of all sizes. Here, as in the Highlands of Scotland, it's possible that the unidentified denizens of the loughs move from one to another. Such migration would help explain why so many very small stretches of water in Connemara seem to house so many animals and such large ones to boot. But there seem to be several kinds of the creatures, if the witnesses' reports are accurate.

In the evening of 22 February 1968, farmer Stephen Coyne and his son were gathering peat beside Lough Nahooin, a tiny peat tarn, only some 100 by 80 yds in extent, near Gladdaghduff. Alerted to something weird in the water by the behaviour of their dog, Coyne sent the boy to fetch the rest of his family to watch it. The seven-strong family were joined by four other local children.

They agreed that the creature was probably about 12 ft long, hairless, with 'eel-like' black skin. It had a 'pole-like' neck, in diameter about 12 in, and apparently horns on its head that may have been protuberances housing its eyes, and a pale mouth. When it put its head underwater two humps showed above the surface. The group caught only glimpses of a tail.

This is entirely different from the animal spotted in Lough Dubh, another small lake in County Galway, near Glinsk. Three men saw a monster there in 1956, and in 1960 three of them were seen in the lough. One day in March 1962, schoolteacher Alphonsus Mullaney and his son Alphonsus Jr went fishing there for pike, and took rod and line stout enough to

Below: *Joseph W. Zarzynski, director of the research group Lake Champlain Phenomena Investigation, prepares sonar equipment in the hope of tracking 'Champ', the lake's famous but mysteriously elusive inhabitant.*

Above: *A model of Ogopogo, the monster of Lake Okanagan in British Columbia, Canada. Local Indian lore acknowledged the creature centuries before it was first sighted by European settlers.*

handle these hefty fish. Mullaney caught more than a fish:

'Suddenly there was a tugging on the line. I thought it might be on a root, so I took it gently. It did not give. I hauled it slowly ashore, and the line snapped. I was examining the line when the lad screamed.

'Then I saw the animal. It was not a seal or anything I had ever seen. It had for instance short thick legs, and a hippo face. It was as big as a cow or an ass, square faced, with small ears and a white pointed horn on its snout. It was dark grey in colour, and covered with bristles or short hair, like a pig.'

The thing, hurt and furious, was trying to get out of the water and wreak vengeance on its hapless fishers. Mullaney and his son fled. A posse of local men later returned with guns to search for the creature, but they found nothing. Nothing like it has been reported since from Lough Dubh.

Different again was the monster seen in Lough Auna, 3 miles or so north-east of Clifden, the 'capital' of Connemara. Air Commodore Kort, who had moved to Ireland after retiring from the Royal Netherlands Air Force, was about to go indoors at the end of a barbecue party in the summer of 1980 when he and one of his guests saw what seemed to be the sawtooth,

reptilian dorsal fin of an animal moving slowly across the lough. The fin was about 5 ft long and stood 12 in out of the water. 'The uncanny thing about it,' said Kort, 'was the gliding movement without any disturbance of the water on the surface.'

WATER SERPENT

In North America, monsters such as the frequently seen but so far unidentified inhabitant of New Brunswick's Lake Utopia and 'Manipogo' of Lake Manitoba in Canada, and those of Lake Erie (where there were many sightings in 1991) and Flathead Lake in Montana, were all locally renowned long before 'Nessie' grabbed the world's headlines.

One such lives in the 109 mile long Lake Champlain, which adjoins New York State, Vermont and Quebec. Lake Champlain's monster, nicknamed 'Champ', has been sighted over 240 times, nearly half of them since 1982. The first really detailed report came in July 1883. The Sheriff of Clinton County, New York, Captain Nathan H. Mooney, was on the north-west arm of the lakeshore when he saw a huge water serpent about 50 yds from him. The creature rose about 5 ft out of the water, which was rough. He reckoned the animal was 25 or 30 ft long. Its neck was about 7 in in diameter, with visibly contracting muscles, and was curved like that 'of a goose when about to take flight'. Mooney noted that there were round white spots inside the creature's mouth.

Candidates for the identity of 'Champ' are identical to those offered for the Loch Ness monster, with the plesiosaur leading.

There are a number of photographs of the creature. Perhaps the most significant was taken on 5 July 1977 by Sandra Mansi of Connecticut, who described the thing as a 'dinosaur' with its neck and head some 6 ft out of the water. The Mansi photograph has been examined by scientists and declared to be a genuine original of something in the water. But what?

THE 'REMORSEFUL ONE'

The best-known Canadian lake monster, 'Ogopogo' of British Columbia's Lake Okanagan, also made its debut long before Nessie. Reports go back to 1850, although

Above: An early effort to trap the creature of Loch Ness – a huge steel cage, built in 1933.

the local Indians were familiar with the beast long before that, and indeed named it the 'remorseful one'. Indian legend says the creature was once human – a murderer turned into a serpent as punishment for his crimes. In 1926, the editor of the Vancouver *Sun* wrote of the creature: 'Too many reputable people have seen it to ignore the seriousness of actual facts.'

A recent sighting shows how witnesses are convinced that there is indeed something odd in Lake Okanagan. In the summer of 1989, hunting guide Ernie Giroux and his wife were standing on the banks of the lake when an animal about 15 ft long surfaced from the calm waters and swam 'real gracefully and fast', as Giroux later told reporters. The creature had a round head 'like a football'. Several feet of the creature's neck and body came up out of the water. The Girouxs saw the monster at the same spot where, a few

weeks before, British Columbian car salesman Ken Chaplin had taken a video of what he described as a dark green, snake-like creature about 15 ft long.

Wildlife experts who saw the video said the animal was more likely a beaver or a large river otter than a 'monster'. Ernie Giroux was unimpressed.

'I've seen a lot of animals swimming in the wild and what we saw that night was definitely not a beaver,' he said bluntly.

At the other end of the Americas is 'Nahuelito', the denizen of Nahuel Huapi Lake at the foot of the Patagonian mountains in southern Argentina. The lake, which covers 318 square miles, is in a popular resort area. Dozens of tourists and local people have seen the creature.

Accounts of the animal vary. Some describe a giant water snake with humps and fish-like fins; others speak of a swan with a snake's head, while yet others liken

THE BEAST HAD ONCE BEEN HUMAN.

Operation Deepscan (below) in 1987 was a massive attempt to 'catch' Nessie. A score or so of launches equipped with sonar detectors made a sweep of the entire Loch. Such a method may, however, have succeeded only in frightening any animals below into hiding.

it to the overturned hull of a boat or a tree stump. Estimates of the creature's length range from 15 to 150 ft. 'Nahuelito' seems to surface only in the summer, when the wind is still. A sudden swell of water and a shooting spray usually precede a sighting.

Patagonia, mountainous and desolate at best, has long been the source of tales of monstrous animals, and even human giants. Patagonian Indians told the first colonists of a huge lake-dwelling creature without head, legs or tail. The rumoured existence of a Patagonian plesiosaur was given additional fuel in the early 1920s, when a gold prospector named Sheffield followed an unusual spoor and found a bizarre water beast at the end of the trail:

'I saw in the middle of the lake,' he reported, 'an animal with a huge neck like that of a swan, and the movement in the water made me suppose the beast to have a body like that of a crocodile.' An expedition, led by Dr C. Onelli, director of the Buenos Aires Zoo, set out to catch or photograph the animal, but sadly failed.

THE LATEST TECHNOLOGIES

What would solve the mystery of the world's lake monsters?

Naturalists are agreed that only the capture of a live specimen or the discovery of a carcass (scientists tend to disapprove of investigators 'acquiring' dead specimens by ballistic means) would admit the monsters into the charmed circle of conventional science. But hunting lake monsters is not the world's easiest task. No live monsters have been caught, yet.

No carcasses have been found either that might be anything other than recognizable animals. Dead specimens may be elusive because the typical monster haunt is a very deep lake. A dead monster would sink to the bottom, where the water pressure would slow down the rate of decomposition – leaving time for eels and other creatures to consume the remains.

Giant nets, submarines, underwater cameras, sonar, lake and loch-side crews of observers have all failed to come up with unambiguous and unimpeachable evidence that would prove to the world that there is an actual monster in any of their reputed haunts. If the animals as reported do exist, they are quite possibly frightened away by the sounds made by the very devices that are being used to track them – as well as by engine noise from the boats.

But until that solid evidence turns up, these strange animals will remain classic mysteries. And credible witnesses will continue to report them, take fuzzy photographs, and keep the lake monster legends alive and swimming.

NOT QUITE HUMAN

Modern reports of strange, over-sized, ape-like wild men have mainly come from the Himalayan mountains, China, Australia, and the American Pacific Northwest, but they are also part of European folklore. In England the creatures were called woodwoses (previous page, carved into the font in Sibton church, Suffolk, and far right).

As he began his descent down the mountain through the heavy mist, the professor thought he was hearing the echo of his footsteps. Terror seized him when he realized that the footsteps belonged to something different – to something malignant...

Abominable snowmen and other horrid hairy man-beasts are strictly contained in the Himalayas, the wilderness of the USA, and the remoter parts of China. Or so you thought.

At 4296 ft Ben MacDhui is the highest peak in Scotland's Cairngorm mountains, and the second highest in the country. Many who have scaled Ben MacDhui are convinced that a malignant entity – which locals call *Am Fear Liath Mor*, the Big Grey Man – lives on the mountain.

The first report from anyone outside the area that something sinister haunted Ben MacDhui came in December 1925 at the Annual General Meeting of the Cairngorm Club. Professor Norman Collie told his suitably astonished audience that in 1891 he had been climbing through heavy mist down from the summit of Ben MacDhui, when, he said, 'I began to think I heard

Right: The Blue Mountains of New South Wales, Australia, which are said to be the haunt of the yowie, the antipodean version of the mysterious man-beast.

something else than merely the noise of my own footsteps. For every few steps I took I heard a crunch, and then another crunch as if someone was walking after me but taking steps three or four times the length of my own.'

At first he thought his imagination was working overtime, but the sound persisted, although whatever was making it remained hidden in the mist. Then, as the eerie crunching continued, Collie said, 'I was seized with terror and took to my heels, staggering blindly among the boulders for four or five miles.'

Collie vowed never to return to the mountain alone, and remained convinced that there was 'something very queer about the top of Ben MacDhui'.

His chilling account was soon picked up by the newspapers, with the result that other mountaineers came forward to record that they too had had similar experiences of uncontrollable and inexplicable fear and panic while on Ben MacDhui. Some had barely managed to avoid lethal falls in their compulsion to get away as quickly as possible from the terrifying presence.

This sounds like a paranormal presence, but some witnesses have actually seen the thing, reporting a huge, man-like figure, and many accounts mention the same heavy footsteps with the unusually long stride that Collie heard.

Plenty of explanations have been put forward for these experiences. They range from the presence of yeti-like man-beasts and optical illusions to the (inevitable) 'base for extraterrestrial aliens' and (more plausibly) hallucinations brought on by lack of oxygen. This latter most probably accounts for some of the more exotic reports of the Big Grey Man, which mention strains of ghostly music and sepulchral laughter wafting across the mountain during its appearance.

But leaving the wonkier propositions aside does not mean dumping the 'man-beast' explanation entirely. There is a long tradition that hairy man-beasts inhabited the British mainland in the past. Known as 'woodwoses', or more mundanely as 'wild men of the woods', their images can be seen carved into the decorations in many old East Anglian churches. There is not much forest on Ben MacDhui, and it is a long way from East Anglia, but the

possibility that a colony of these legendary creatures has survived in Scotland remains to tantalize the imagination.

FOUL ODOURS

Although conventional zoology says that one wouldn't expect to find apes of any kind, let alone 'ape men', living in South America or Australia, any more than in the British Isles, both continents can boast plenty of eyewitnesses who would swear that the contrary is true and that the scientists are wrong.

Australia's man-beast is known as the 'yowie'. Most reports have come from

HIS CHILLING ACCOUNT WAS SOON CORROBORATED BY OTHER FRIGHTENED MOUNTAINEERS.

Below: *The enigmatic female beast shot by members of a geological survey team led by François de Loys on the Venezuela–Colombia border in 1920. Controversy still rages over the true nature of the creature.*

HERE WAS CONCLUSIVE PHYSICAL PROOF AT LAST – THE CARCASS OF THE FEMALE BEAST.

New South Wales and Queensland, and the creatures have been seen by settlers since the mid-19th century at least. The Aborigines have known about them since long before then. Like North America's 'bigfoot' and 'sasquatch', the yowie can remain remarkably unperturbed when surprised. When George Summerell, who was riding a horse, came upon one bending down to drink from a creek near Bemboka, New South Wales, on 12 October 1912, it simply 'rose to its full height, of about 7 feet, and looked quietly at the horseman', according to an item in the Sydney *Morning Herald.* 'Then stooping down again, it finished its drink, and then, picking up a stick that lay by it, walked steadily away...and disappeared among the rocks and timber 150 yards away.'

Footprints around the shore of the creek showed that the creature had been there at least a fortnight before, as well, and that the animal had only four toes – a feature of other man-beast prints taken around the world. But the yowie has two other features commonly reported by witnesses of the North American man-beasts: no neck, and the ability to emit revolting smells at will.

In early 1978, an Australian National Parks worker was cutting timber near Springbrook in Queensland when he saw 'this big black hairy man-thing' about 12 ft away from him.

'It had huge hands,' he said, 'and...a flat, black shiny face, with two big yellow eyes and a hole for a mouth. It just stared at me and I stared back. I was so numb I couldn't even raise the axe I had in my hand. We [were] staring at each other for about 10 minutes before it suddenly gave off a foul smell that made me vomit – then it just made off sideways and disappeared.'

THE BEASTS ATTACK

The most intriguing and controversial encounter with a South American man-beast took place along the Tarra River on the Venezuela–Colombia border in 1920. A 20-strong team of geological surveyors, led by Swiss geologist Dr François de Loys, had set out in 1917 but at the end of three years had been reduced to a handful by disease, venomous animals, and the poisoned arrows of hostile Indians. One day in 1920, this ragged band saw coming through the foliage ahead of them two 5 ft tall, ape-like but tail-less creatures, walking upright on their hind legs.

When the beasts – one male and the other female – saw the geologists, they became plainly agitated, tearing angrily at the vegetation around them. They got so excited that both defecated into their hands and flung their excrement at the scientists. Then they moved forward – as if to attack, it seemed to the geologists, who responded with a hail of small-arms fire. The female died instantly. The male fled.

The geologists examined the carcass, noted its details, and photographed it. Most of the pictures were lost when the party's boat capsized later in the expedition, but one survived. On returning to Europe, De Loys showed it to the French anthropologist Professor George Montandon. He was convinced that it showed a species comparable to the Old World's apes – chimpanzees, gorillas, orang-utans and gibbons. He formally named it *Amerantropoides loysi* – 'Loys's American ape'. Other scientists were less impressed.

The creature did look somewhat like an over-sized and tail-less spider monkey, and

Below: *It was in tropical jungle like this that De Loys and his party came upon and shot at a pair of aggressive man-beasts in 1920.*

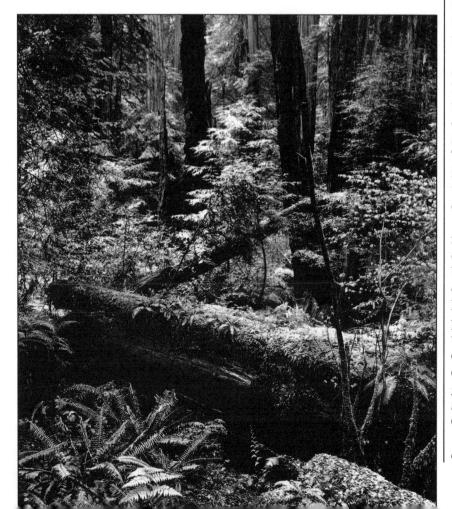

most zoologists maintained that it was some form of spider monkey. Some even hinted, none too subtly, at a hoax. Montandon answered all the criticisms in painstaking detail, but his critics were unmoved: as far as establishment science was concerned, De Loys's find was not an ape, and the issue was soon simply ignored.

But there is plenty of circumstantial evidence in favour of creatures like the one De Loys shot and photographed. Indian tribes in the jungles all over South America have long believed in the existence of ape-like beasts that walk upright and lack tails. And among the ruins of various South American and Mexican ancient cities are sculptures of gorilla-like creatures quite unlike any known New World primate – but they do resemble the South American ape woman shot by De Loys's party. Further, there is no ecological reason why such an ape should not be able to survive in the South American environment – but conventional science always prefers to ignore awkward little questions and hair-splitting logic like that.

OUT OF AFRICA

In contrast to the areas we've looked at so far, it would make sense if hairy man-beasts were to be found living in Africa. Apart from its vast areas of wilderness in which such creatures could roam free, with little risk of being detected by people, the continent is now known to be the 'cradle of mankind' – the place where humans, *homo sapiens*, evolved.

The oldest African fossils of hominids are the australopithecines, which first appeared over three million years ago. Some types were notably slender, others more robust – and so it is just possible that these or other ancient evolutionary forms, somewhere between apes and men, have survived out of sight in Africa to this day. And if one goes by the huge dossier of eyewitness reports, Africa is indeed home to an enormous variety of unidentified man-beasts.

Living specimens of slender australopithecine would look like several unidentified man-beasts as witnesses have described them. Among these are Zaïre's 'kakundakari', the 'fating'ho' of Senegal, and Tanzania's 'agogwe'. According to

Above: *Cryptozoologist Loren Coleman, who was the first to note the extraordinary similarity of the environments in China and the USA where man-beasts have been sighted.*

witnesses, the agogwe is small, russet-furred, and man-like, and sometimes mixes with other primates such as baboons. Elders of the Mandinka tribe of Senegal speak of the fating'ho as if it were just as real as any of the known animals inhabiting their lands, though it is rarely seen nowadays (perhaps simply because it has become rarer).

Other man-beasts seem to resemble the robust species of australopithecines. Among these are the 'kikomba' of Zaïre, and Sudan's 'wa'ab'. These may even be surviving examples of humanity's direct evolutionary ancestor, *Homo erectus*.

The French anthropologist Jacqueline Roumeguere-Eberhardt has concluded that there are no less than five different species of man-beast living in Kenya. She has cautiously dubbed them 'X One' through to 'X Five'.

X One is a typical bigfoot-like being, hairy, huge, and possibly social, since it's been seen carrying buffalo meat rather than gorging it on the spot. It also defends itself with a kind of sardonic gentleness. A young hunter who was cornered by the beast said it simply removed his arrows from their quiver, broke them up and put them back.

Right: *One of over 1000 footprints apparently made by a company of bigfoot near Bossburg, Washington State, in 1969. The creature's deformed foot was over 16 in long.*

Below: *Two prospectors made these sketches of their sighting of a sasquatch near Pitt Lake, British Columbia, on 28 June 1965.*

X Two is a cave-dwelling creature with a hairless, beige-coloured body with curly black hair on its head. A noticeably human-oid beast, it is tall and thin, and seems to live in nuclear families.

X Three is tall, and uses tools for hunting. Males have been seen to fell buffalo 'with an uprooted tree with its roots carved into spikes'. The beast then wields 'a spear-like knife' to cut out its prey's internal organs, 'which are then eaten on the spot'.

X Four is a hairy-chested, fat-bodied pygmy-like hominoid that, witnesses say, is often to be seen carrying a digging stick, which it uses to uproot tubers.

X Five is exclusively vegetarian, a man-beast that carries bows and arrows and is apparently capable of making leatherwork bags.

Despite the wealth of sightings of African man-beasts, no one has yet caught

or killed one, or found a skeleton that would provide conclusive proof of their existence. But Africa has given zoologists plenty of surprises in the 20th century alone. As the saying goes, 'There is always something new out of Africa.' So, perhaps, as the English cryptozoologist Dr Karl Shuker has put it, the most secretive of continents may be saving its most sensational surprise for the future.

THE INCREDIBLE HULK?

As far as the West is concerned, the grand-daddy of all hairy man-beasts is, of course, the so-called 'abominable snowman' or 'yeti' of the Himalayas. The existence of what, correctly translated, the local people call 'a man-like living thing that is not a human being' first came to the West's attention in 1921, when Lt-Col C.K. Howard-Bury was surveying Mt Everest for a forthcoming attempt to reach the summit. On 22 September that year he came across huge footprints on a snowfield where, earlier, he had seen dark, man-like forms moving around. News of these two events sped round the world, and have been reinforced by sightings from virtually every mountaineering expedition into the area since.

The term 'abominable snowman' is not only a mistranslation of the Nepalese term for these creatures – it's irritatingly misleading. There seems to be nothing particularly abominable about the yeti, and they appear on the high Himalayan snowfields only when making their way from one hot and humid valley, where they seem to spend most of their time, to another. And the term also implies that there is only one of these creatures. Not only are there many individuals, if reports are to be trusted, but there are at least three different kinds of yeti.

The word yeti itself is a Sherpa term that means, roughly, 'That-thing-there'. Investigator (and oil millionaire) Tom Slick was the first to conclude, from his expeditions to the Himalayas in 1957 and 1958, that there were at least two types of creature that local people had seen.

The 'original' yeti is the *meh-teh*, a man-sized creature that sports a conical head set on a stout neck, with a jutting jaw and a wide, lipless mouth. The body is covered in thick, reddish-brown fur. Prints show short, broad feet. Meh-teh eat plants and small animals, including birds, which they hunt in the upper forests of the mountains.

There is also a pygmy man-beast of the Himalayas, *teh-lma*, which means 'man-like being'. Standing about 3–4 ft tall, these creatures live deeper in the valleys than meh-teh, surviving on a diet largely of frogs and insects. Their thick fur is dark red, with a slight mane on the back.

The third species of yeti is known in the Himalayas, but only by repute. Called *dzu-teh* – 'hulking living thing' – these beasts are huge, far taller and bulkier than a human, with a dark shaggy coat, a flat head with beetling brows, long powerful arms and hands, and large feet that leave prints with two pads under the first toe, which points out and away from the others on the foot. They live not in the Himalayas but in eastern Tibet and northern China, on a mainly vegetarian diet.

This matter of the two pads (and other features) showing in the dzu-teh's footprint is important, and so is the animal's habitat. American cryptozoologist Loren Coleman first pointed out that both plant and animal species in the areas of China where dzu-teh (called 'yeren' in China) are consistently reported bear an uncanny resemblance – they are often related to, or the same as –

Tracks made by a bigfoot on Blue Creek Mountain, California, in the late summer of 1967 (above left) *were measured by investigator René Dahinden at 15 in* (above).

So, are bigfoot (alias sasquatch) and yeren (alias dzu-teh) related – or even separate communities of the same animal? And if so, what animal?

The favourite candidate is a species of giant ape, named *Gigantopithecus*, which lived in southern China until it – apparently – became extinct 500,000 years ago. Its anatomy is somewhere between ape and human. Gigantopithecus, as its name implies, was huge. Males probably weighed around 800 lb and females around 500 lb. This is easily the largest primate that ever lived. Gigantopithecus also, almost certainly, stood and walked in a human manner.

Humans and all apes share a unique set of anatomical traits in the arms, shoulders, and thorax, since all evolved to swing through trees. Humans gave up this form of personal transport long ago, preferring walking, horse-riding and eventually the Ford Model T. As a result they lost their tails. Gigantopithecus also belonged to this

Above and below: *Frames from the famous movie of a bigfoot filmed by Roger Patterson on 20 October 1967 at Bluff Creek in northern California. Expert opinion says the film was not faked.*

those found in the Pacific Northwest of North America. And this is where bigfoot and sasquatch are most often seen. And the footprints of yeren and bigfoot are strikingly similar in the configuration of their pads, ridges and disposition of the toes.

group of higher primates, but it was too large to swing through trees, and probably, therefore, also lost its tail. Its wide chest, broad shoulders, and lack of tail would make it conspicuous among apes – and remarkably like a human in appearance.

Gigantopitheces had ape-like faces and were covered with body hair. Their faces would have had the ape's retreating forehead and blunt nose, but with a more human set to the mouth and jaw. They did not make tools and had less-than-human intelligence. They probably did not live in close social groups. All these features are remarkably consistent with the reported appearance and behaviour of bigfoot/sasquatch.

Most authorities presume that Gigantopithecus is extinct because the most recent fossil teeth (from northern Vietnam) are 300,000 years old. Other finds date back a million years. But one early Gigantopithecus jaw from India is at least five million years old. Thus, the animals survived for four million years although we have no direct physical evidence that they did. So they could have survived during the 300,000 years since the owner of the most recent fossil remains died off and still leave no sign of being here.

'I RAN OUT OF FILM'

Although many American Indian tribes of the Pacific Northwest tell tales of bigfoot, and in them treat the creature just as they do less elusive animals, it was not until 1958 that the American public at large became aware of the bigfoot phenomenon. In the summer of 1958 strange, giant footprints cropped up around some road-making equipment at Bluff Creek in northern California. The tracks appeared several nights in a row, alarming the workers who found them. Once the major San Francisco papers picked up the story, it soon got national attention. Bigfoot had become the ultimate reclusive media star.

The next major sighting, which also netted a major piece of evidence, came in 1967. On 20 October that year Roger Patterson and Bob Gimlin of Yakima, Washington, went to Bluff Creek in the hope of catching sight of a bigfoot after hearing that tracks had been seen again in the area. They went on horseback, and

were 40 or 50 miles from the nearest road when they rounded a bend on the trail and came to a creek. In Gimlin's words: 'Here this thing stood by the creek, just stood. We were on one side of the creek, the creature on the other and our horses went crazy. Roger's little horse just went bananas.'

Patterson managed to haul out the 16-mm movie camera, loaded with colour film, that he was carrying in his saddlebag.

'This creature turned,' said Gimlin, 'and started to walk away from us, just slow like a man would if he were just walking down the street, but as it did this, Roger ran across the creek behind it, but then he stumbled on a sandbar…He was shooting the camera while he was running. He hollered back for me when he stumbled and fell. He said, "Cover me!" and, naturally, I knew what he meant.

'So I rode across the creek on my horse and took my .30-06 rifle out of the saddle scabbard and just stood there (pointing but not aiming the rifle at the beast). When I did this, this creature was…about 90 feet [away] – and it turned and looked at me; just turned as it was walking away. It never stopped walking. And then…I heard Roger say, "Oh, my God, I ran out of film."'

Above: *Bob Gimlin, who was with Patterson at Bluff Creek, holds two casts that the pair made of tracks left by the bigfoot. The prints measured over 14 in long.*

'ROGER'S LITTLE HORSE JUST WENT BANANAS.'

Above: *Detailed drawing of the Bluff Creek bigfoot's head, made by Russian researcher Dmitri Baynov after studying the movie.*

FORTY POLICE SPECIALISTS WERE FORCED TO CONCLUDE THAT THE FOOTPRINTS WERE MADE BY A GENUINE BIGFOOT.

Below: *Leading US bigfoot researcher Grover Krantz, with a cast of a bigfoot print.*

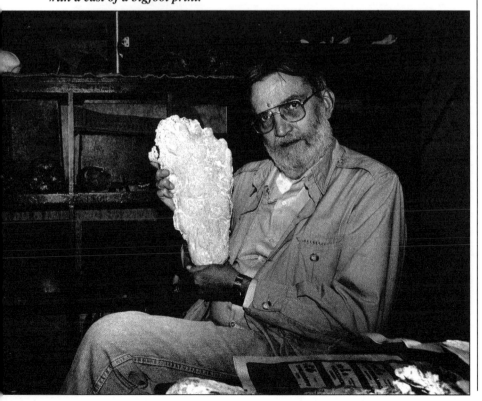

Gimlin remains adamant that he and Patterson saw a genuine bigfoot that day. Two things support his contention. First, Patterson is now dead, and Gimlin has more to gain financially from a confession to a hoax than stoutly maintaining the opposite – after all, he owns no rights in the film.

Second, the oft-mentioned possibility that a third party hoaxed the two bigfoot-hunters seems highly unlikely. To begin with, such a prankster would have had to have anticipated the pair's moves over many miles of rough country, seeing them but not being seen. Even if the hypothetical hoaxer had managed that feat of fieldcraft, only an idiot would risk getting in the way of a shot from Gimlin's powerful hunting rifle; the .30-06 round will down a bear.

And some expert scientific opinion backs the men's claim. One expert who studied the film, Dmitri Donskoy, Professor of Biomechanics at the Soviet Central Institute of Physical Culture in Moscow, noted that the creature's gait was that of an animal with enormous weight and strength, and that the movement of the whole body was fluid and confident. 'These factors…allow us to evaluate the gait of the creature as a natural movement without any sign of the artfulness that one would see in an imitation,' he concluded. 'At the same time, with all the diversity of locomotion illustrated by the creature of the footage, its gait as seen is absolutely non-typical of man.'

Another expert, Donald Grieve, Reader in Biomechanics at the Royal Free Hospital in London, was similarly impressed, but had a reservation. He felt that if the camera speed – which Patterson did not know for sure – had been set at 24 frames per second, the film could be showing a large, walking man. But if the film had been shot at 18 frames per second, no human being would be able to match the movements shown. He concluded with rare honesty: 'My subjective impressions have oscillated between total acceptance of the Bigfoot on the grounds that the film would be difficult to fake, to one of irrational rejection based on an emotional response to the possibility that the Bigfoot actually exists.'

The leading US authority on bigfoot, Professor Grover Krantz of Washington State University, made a detailed analysis of the movie in 1991, and concluded that it was indeed shot at 18 frames per second. The animal's movements, he believes, were impossible for a human to imitate, and convincingly show the creature's massiveness and strength. And he noted that its huge size, and muscles to match, were well outside the normal range of human variation. In other words, if Patterson's bigfoot had been a man in a fur suit, he would have been a giant who had pumped an awful lot of iron.

DEAD OR ALIVE

More impressive evidence for the reality of bigfoot comes from a set of footprints that were discovered and cast by US Forest Service workers in 1982, in the Blue Mountains along the Washington–Oregon border. The prints were made in very fine soil that was slightly damp. All the casts show ridges on the skin under the toes and on the soles. These are just like fingerprints, and only the palms and soles of higher primates have them. Forty police fingerprinters have studied these casts over the years, and have all concluded that the footprints must have been made by one or more genuine bigfeet.

Opinion among anthropologists and primatologists who have seen the casts is mixed. Many suggested that the casts had been made from human footprints that had somehow been enlarged – a latex mould of a footprint will expand by 50 per cent when soaked in kerosene. This trick also expands the spacing between the ridges by 50 per cent. All the fingerprint experts noted that the ridges on these footprints were spaced just like those on the skin of other primates.

Despite all this circumstantial evidence, the only thing that will convince mainstream science of the reality of bigfoot will be part or all of a specimen itself, dead or alive. Professor Krantz remarks that 'a single lower jaw would be enough to establish not only its existence, but whether Gigantopithecus is still with us'.

INFESTED WATERS

Bigfoot is by no means the only mystery man-beast in North America, nor the strangest. The prize for the most bizarre has to go to a nightmarish creature nicknamed Lizard Man.

Witnesses describe it as 7 ft tall, walking upright like a man – but with green scaly skin, glowing red eyes, three toes on each foot and three fingers – each sprouting a 4 in long claw – on each hand. This grotesque animal, or apparition, first introduced itself to humanity around 2 am on 29 June 1988, near Scape Ore Swamp, outside the one-horse town of Bishopville in Lee County, South Carolina.

Seventeen-year-old Christopher Davis had just finished changing a flat tyre on his car when he saw 'something large' running toward him across a nearby field. As the creature came nearer, Davis leaped into the vehicle and tried to slam the door – only to see the thing seize it and try to wrench it open. Davis had plenty of time – more than he would have liked – to note the fine details of its unlovely appearance. Davis eventually got the car going and made his getaway. When he got home, shaking with fright, he found long scratches on the car roof, and the wing mirror in serious disarray.

Others encountered Lizard Man that summer, but none helped solve the mystery of what the creature was. However, records show that scaly and apparently aquatic man-beasts have been reported before, in many parts of North America.

Such creatures sound like a fantasy, or a hoax, or merely the effect on surprised witnesses of a person in a diving suit. But there is an odd twist to the Lizard Man tale, especially if one bears in mind the possibility that bigfoot and its international relations may be a surviving form of the officially extinct Gigantopithecus. In 1982, paleontologists Drs Dale A. Russell and R. Séguin of the Canadian National Museum of Natural Sciences published a paper in which they set out what a dinosaurian equivalent of a human being may have looked like, had the dinosaurs survived to the present. They suggest it would have been a two-legged creature with three-fingered hands, and in general would have looked startlingly like Lizard Man.

THE 'HUMAN DINOSAUR' ATTACKED WITH A VICIOUS FEROCITY.

Below: *As shown by this artist's impression, bigfoot towers over an average-sized man.*

MONSTERS FROM THE DEEP

Since pre-Biblical times, sailors have returned home from long voyages with tales of huge monsters and cunning sea serpents. Many stories can be attributed to the lonely nights at sea, and alcoholic solace, but should these include the testimony of senior naval officers, and the uniden-tifiable carcasses washed up upon remote shores?

'He had a large body and a small alligator-like head. The neck seemed to be medium size, matching the size of the head. The body was very large, shaped somewhat like a seal. There was a mane of bristly hair or fur which ran down the middle of his head.

'He would surface the upper part of his body and glide out of the water with the lower part of his body remaining submerged. The portion of his body which was visible measured about 40 feet in length. We estimate his weight to be between 35 and 40 tons over all.

'At no time did the whole body show. He stayed on the surface no longer than 40 seconds at a time. You could hear the heavy weight of his upper body when he dove below, creating a large splash and a subsequent wake. He surfaced four times in 20 minutes during which we were trying to stay clear of him. The Captain changed course to steer away from him and the queer fellow surfaced on our starboard beam…

'Another peculiar thing about him was that when he'd surface he would turn his head looking towards us and it seemed to us he was playful and curious. Another point was that on the upper part of his body there were two flippers, similar to those of a seal.'

So runs part of a report of a sea-monster sighting on 3 September 1959 by the cook, Joseph H. Bourassa, of the scalloper *Noreen*. The ship was 120 miles out from Bermuda, east of Pollock. Bourassa had been at sea for 20 years, and had never before seen anything like what he saw that day.

'IT SEEMED TO US HE WAS PLAYFUL AND CURIOUS.'

Opposite: *A 16th-century artist's rendering of a sea serpent. Of the thousands of such creatures that have been sighted over the centuries, surprisingly few conform to this stereotype. Sea serpents are as bewildering in their variety as in every other aspect of their existence.*

Below: *A German U-boat of World War 1 vintage. When one such craft torpedoed a British freighter, a 60 ft long sea serpent was blown out of the water at the same time.*

Morgawr, the Cornish sea serpent, as photographed by witness 'Mary F.' in early February 1976. Although much smaller, the animal bears a distinct resemblance to many descriptions and photographs of the Loch Ness monster.

Right: *Strong drink and sailors have always been boon companions. Some of the wilder reports of monsters seen at sea may fairly be put down to the effects of the demon booze.*

NAVAL REPORTS

What are sea monsters? How many kinds of them are there? Compare Bourassa's account with this, from an officer of the Imperial German Navy who was aboard the U-boat U28 when, during World War 1, the submarine blew the British *Iberian* out of the water in the North Atlantic:

'A little later pieces of wreckage, and among them a gigantic sea-animal, writhing and struggling wildly, were shot out of the water to a height of 60 to 100 feet…the animal sank out of sight after 10 or 15 seconds… It was about 60 feet long, was like a crocodile in shape and had four limbs with powerful webbed feet and a long tail tapering to a point.'

If this creature bears little enough resemblance to the animal in the first account quoted, try this one:

'Then I saw this great eel-like monster rear its head like a Scotch terrier struck by curiosity. Its eyes were red and green, like the port and starboard lights of a ship. It was about ninety feet long. As we approached within 200 feet, it rose out of the water, with its seven humps like a camel and its face like a cow, and didn't make any noise, but I thought it should have mooed. Then it uttered an eerie bellow, like a bull whale in its last agony and reared up, perhaps thirty feet, perhaps fifty, and flopped over on its back. Along its flanks was a phosphorescent glow. By this time we had five searchlights on it, and it turned to the side and dived.'

The report came from First Officer A.E. Richards, who witnessed the episode from the bridge of the liner *Santa Lucia* in the long thin dawn light of 21 October 1933. The ship was off Sheringham Point near Victoria, in Cadboro Bay, Vancouver Island, British Columbia. The bay is famous for its resident sea monster 'Caddy' or, more pretentiously, *Cadborosaurus*.

One more example will drive home the point to which we are making so laborious a pilgrimage:

'It looked like an elephant waving its trunk, but the trunk was a long neck with a small head on the end, like a snake's head. It had humps on the back which moved in a funny way. The colour was black or very dark brown, and the skin seemed to be like a sealion's…the animal frightened me… I do not like the way it moved when it was swimming.'

'The animal' is called *morgawr*, the Cornish Celtic word for 'sea giant'. It made many appearances off the Cornish coast in the 1970s, and this particular witness, known only as Mary F., actually managed to photograph it, in February 1976, as it played in the sea off Rosemullion Head near Falmouth. The creature bears a striking resemblance to the popular image of the Loch Ness monster, and for all anyone knows may be of the same family, although Mary F. estimated its length to be no more than 15–18 ft – a veritable infant beside Nessie, and a positive midget compared to the monstrous 'eel-like' animal that First Officer Richards saw disporting itself off Vancouver Island.

PANDORA'S BOX

And there lies the rub. On the face of it, no one sea monster seems to bear much likeness to another. So what are we dealing with? The usual catalogue of possibilities and explanations presents itself unbidden – hallucinations, misidentifications, bored sailors livening up a ship's log to bemuse posterity, tired and emotional witnesses (considerably less of a rarity at sea than monster sightings: many long-haul freighters are navigated through a sea-fog of alcohol).

Or are we back in the world of officially extinct or simply officially overlooked animals? There is some reason to believe that some apparently extinct creatures have survived in the sea. The ostensibly fresh-water Loch Ness monster, for instance, may be a marine animal, a surviving plesiosaur, that merely visits the Loch on occasion. On the evidence, there is no compelling reason to suppose for an instant that scientists have catalogued all the animals that live in the world's oceans. The waters, after all, cover roughly two-thirds of the surface of the Earth, and they keep on presenting little surprises to our friends

in the laboratory coats. Just to cite three examples: in 1958, a previously unknown species of porpoise, now called the 'cochito', was found in the Gulf of California; eight years later 'megamouth' was discovered, hauled up on the anchor of an Hawaiian survey ship – a shark so different from other sharks that zoologists had to create an entire new family to accommodate it, and it duly entered the record books, too, as the third largest known species of its kind; and in 1983 a new species of killer whale, the Prudes Bay, peculiar to the Antarctic, was added to zoology's roll of honour.

Honest scientists know that they have not plumbed the depths of the riches of life hidden in the oceans. The same honesty makes their hair, quite rightly, stand on end at the thought that untold biological riches are being destroyed in the Amazon rainforests every day. Biologists do not know what we may be losing as the fires of greed consume trees, herbs, insects, mammals and birds by the square mile every minute. They only know such a vast and fecund area must be a living treasure house. So it is with the seas of the world.

Above: *This shot of Earth from space shows just how much of the surface of the planet is covered by water. With millions of square miles of ocean unfrequented by humanity, it would be astonishing if there were no rare and unusual animals still unknown to science.*

THE SEAS ARE VAST – AND TREACHEROUS.

There have to be creatures there waiting, willingly or not, to be discovered, but the seas of the world are harder, vaster, more expensive and more treacherous to explore than any rainforest, and that is the scientists' problem.

MONSTERS OF THE BIBLICAL SEAS

Our problem, for the time being – perhaps in the forlorn hope of persuading scientists to recognize that there is a potentially fruitful field of research waiting to be taken up – is to make sense of such material as we have. There is plenty of circumstantial evidence that sea monsters exist: but how good is it? Leaving aside the mistakes, hallucinations, hoaxes and misperceptions of drunken sailors, we are left with two basic possibilities as to the origin or reality of sea monsters.

First is the possibility that some, at least, of the reported sightings are of animals that have survived their official 'extinction'. Second is the possibility that these are creatures – some rare, some perhaps less so – that have simply eluded the eyes of science. They are not 'unknown' or 'unexplained' animals, but simply unidentified ones.

Whatever we are dealing with, there is nothing new about them. Large and terrifying animals have been known to exist since Old Testament times, and from the days before those ancient texts were written as well. Jonah was swallowed by a 'whale'. The other monster of the Biblical seas, Leviathan, is also mentioned in greater or lesser detail in various places in the Psalms of David, and the Books of Isaiah and Job. One senses that these passages reveal what only the Lord can know of creatures that swim beneath the face of the deep.

'HUGEST OF LIVING CREATURES'

The most extensive description of Leviathan comes in Chapter 41 of that dark, bejewelled hymn to an ancient existentialism, the Book of Job. In this, the Lord continues to upbraid Job for his presumptions, and paints a picture of such power that one cannot help feeling not only that the passage seems to be celebrating the tremendous vitality of this creature, but that it is revered even by the one that created it:

'Canst thou draw out leviathan with an hook? or his tongue with a cord which thou lettest down?

Wilt thou play with him as with a bird? or wilt thou bind him for thy maidens?

Shall the companions make a banquet of him? shall they part him among the merchants?

Lay thine hand upon him, remember the battle, do no more.

Behold, the hope of him is in vain; shall not one be cast down even at the sight of him?

None is so fierce that dare stir him up...

Who can open the doors of his face? his teeth are terrible round about.

His scales are his pride, shut up together as with a close seal.

The flakes of his flesh are joined together: they are firm in themselves; they cannot be moved.

When he raiseth himself up, the mighty are afraid: by reason of breakings they purify themselves.

He esteemeth iron as straw, and brass as rotten wood.

Below: *Jonah is regurgitated from the belly of the 'whale' – clearly not a conventional whale since, despite their size, these huge sea-going mammals are not capable of swallowing anything as large as a man.*

The arrow cannot make him flee: sling-stones are turned with him into stubble.

He maketh the deep to boil like a pot: he maketh the sea like a pot of ointment.

He maketh a path to shine after him; one would think the deep to be hoary.

Upon earth there is not his like, who is made without fear.

He beholdeth all high things: he is a king over all the children of pride.'

All the elements of a sea-monster sighting seem to be here: the terrific size, the sense of its enormous strength and invulnerability, the confident – even casual – indifference of the creature to its puny human observers, and its sheer, awe-inspiring strangeness.

A 17th-century English poet, John Milton, a mere bricklayer in comparison to the Hebrew architect of language, was also entranced by this creature, but he could only grope blindly to recapture the drift of his predecessor's magnificent vision:

'There Leviathan
Hugest of living creatures, on the deep
Stretch'd like a promontory sleeps or swims,
And seems a moving land…'

But what was Leviathan? Can we tell, at this distance in time?

A TWISTED SERPENT

The translators of the Anglican Church's Authorized Version of the Bible appointed by King James did not actually translate the original Hebrew word, which was *livyathan*, probably because they could not connect its meaning to anything they knew in their own world. Literally, it means 'twisted serpent'.

The 5th- or 6th-century BC Jewish poet who recorded the trials of Job seems himself to have had only a sketchy idea of what Leviathan was. The ancient Hebrews, curiously, were not a seafaring nation, although they were always within reach of the Mediterranean sea. Possibly all sea beasts were somewhat mysterious to them, although they would have been aware that some were of unnaturally large size.

The vision of a monstrous sea animal that possessed the poet who wrote the Book of Job was possibly, and in part, derived

Behold now Behemoth which I made with thee

W. Blake invenit & sculpt

from sightings of whales or sharks. The most likely source was probably foreign sailors' accounts of sperm whales, the animals on which the neighbouring Phoenicians – known in the Bible as Canaanites, and living in what is now Lebanon – based their whaling industry.

The Biblical story of Job is based on a Middle Eastern (not Hebrew) legend much older than the poet who re-created it, and his notion of Leviathan was almost certainly influenced by regional tales of dragons. Images of monsters mentioned in the myths of Egypt or Assyria, such as Tiamat and Apophis, would also have influenced the poet's vision. 'Leviathan', then, means any great sea or land monster.

The Belgian zoologist Dr Bernard Heuvelmans, who has made the most detailed study of sea-monster reports in modern times, suggests that Chapter 41 of Job, quoted in part above, suggests not the whale but a melodramatic account of a long-necked sea serpent.

The phrases describing a creature that

Above: *The Lord shows Job the might of Behemoth and Leviathan in William Blake's engraving. Later scientific researchers have come to the same conclusion as the visionary Blake: that Leviathan is a scaly serpent of the sea.*

Right: *Sketches by zoologist Dr Karl Shuker, based on eyewitness Owen Burnham's descriptions, of the weird creature washed up on a Gambian seashore in June 1983. The dead animal was about 15 ft long.*

K.P.N. Shuker

THEY WERE TRYING TO SEVER ITS HEAD.

'raiseth himself' up out of the water and 'beholdeth all high things' certainly suggest an animal with a long neck. And 'the flakes of his flesh [translated elsewhere as 'the members of his body'] are joined together' may be a half-explanatory reference to the sinuous humped appearance of these creatures that (now as then) so many modern reports of sea monsters also mention.

This aspect of Leviathan rather qualifies the possibility that the true source of its reputation is the sperm whale or sharks. This is also the moment to remark on the sceptics' claim that the 'humps' of sea monsters are really a misperception of dolphins leaping in line. This is the kind of dozy (and pretty desperate) rationalization that could only come from people who have never seen dolphins in the sea. They are unmistakable for anything but dolphins.

Was Leviathan no more than a compound of mythical beasts, hearsay, and ignorance? Or was it all that, but with the hearsay relating directly to actual sea monsters? This seems at least possible. Leviathan, then, is at least partly a genuine unidentified creature.

BEEF-RED FLESH

In June 1983, amateur naturalist Owen Burnham was on holiday with his family on the coast of the Gambia, west Africa, taking a break from their home in neighbouring Senegal. During the night of 11/12 June, a large unidentified animal was washed ashore on the beach near where they were staying. They heard about this the following morning. At 8.30 am Burnham, together with his brother and sister and father, went down to the shore to look for the creature. They found it easily enough, along with two Africans who were trying to sever its head so that they could sell the skull to tourists.

The animal was battered, distended with internal gas, and smelled foul, but it was essentially complete and had not begun to decompose. It had not been dead long. Burnham was familiar with all of the major land and sea creatures native to the region, but he was unable to identify this one. The group persuaded the two native entrepreneurs to stop for long enough to let them measure the animal. Burnham, lacking a camera, also made sketches of it and counted the teeth.

The animal was smooth-skinned, with four flippers. One hind flipper had been torn off, and the other damaged. Its overall length was about 15 ft, of which 5 ft were taken up by a long, pointed tail whose cross-section was like a rounded-off triangle.

The animal had a slightly domed forehead, and at the end of its 18 in long snout were what looked like a pair of nostrils. Thinking it might be some form of marine mammal (a whale or dolphin), Burnham looked for a blowhole, but found none. Nor could he see any mammary glands. If there were any male organs they were too damaged to recognize. The creature's long, thin jaws were very tightly closed; Burnham said he had 'a job' to prise them apart. He counted 80 teeth, which he noted were evenly distributed, very sharp, and similar in shape to a barracuda's but whiter and thicker.

The flippers were round and solid. There were no toes, claws or nails. When the Africans returned and completed their work of removing the head, the witnesses could see that the animal's vertebrae were very thick. It took the men 20 minutes' dedicated hacking with a machete to sever it. The animal's flesh was dark red, 'like beef'.

Burnham speaks Mandinka, the local language, fluently and asked the men the name of the animal. They told him *kunthum belein*, Mandinka for 'cutting jaws'; this is what the coastal fishermen call dolphins. Burnham later described the unknown animal to many native fishermen in the area in the hope that they might be able to identify it, but none had ever seen anything like it. He concluded that the butchers on the beach had called it a 'dolphin' because it looked vaguely like one.

Burnham then wrote to various authorities on wildlife to try to get further leads, but got no real help. Most suggested animals that he had already been able to rule out thanks to his familiarity with the denizens of the region.

Burnham also said that he 'looked

> **THE ONLY CREATURES THAT RESEMBLED THE ANIMAL WERE SUPPOSED TO HAVE DIED OUT 60 MILLION YEARS BEFORE.**

Below: *A massive sea serpent was spotted from HMS Daedalus in 1848, and this engraving was based on an eyewitness's drawing sent to the Lords of the Admiralty by Captain M'Quhoe, the ship's commander.*

Right: *A Victorian representation of 'the legendary sea serpent'. The animal seen here would probably now be classified by cryptozoologists as a 'super-eel'.*

Below right: *A giant squid, some 24 ft long, is caught off the Canary Islands by crew of the French gunboat* **Alecton** *on 30 November 1861. Giant squids may well be responsible for many 'monster' sightings at sea.*

'TO SEE SUCH A THING WAS AWESOME.'

through encyclopedias and every book I could lay hands on' in trying to identify the mystery animal. Eventually, he found a photograph of the skull of the extinct Australian *Kronosaurus queenslandicus*, which he felt was the nearest thing he had seen so far. However, he noted that that skull was 10 ft long: clearly it was not the same as the creature he had seen.

AWESOME

Burnham's detailed reports of his find, and the sketches and measurements he made, were analysed at length by zoologist Dr Karl Shuker in the mid-1980s. Shuker rapidly ruled out a number of near-contenders, and realized that the only creatures that at all resembled Burnham's find had long since died out – and, what was more, had been extinct for more than 60 million years. One was the pliosaur, a family of short-necked plesiosaurs that included the *Kronosaurus* whose skull Burnham had recognized but rejected. The other was a group of non-scaly sea crocodiles, called thalattosuchians, who had slender bodies and four paddle-like limbs. Their tails had a dorsal fin, but a thalattosuchian whose fin had been torn off or scuffed away would look amazingly like the beast of Burnham's sketches. And if thalattosuchians had survived into the present, it is possible that they would no longer have such a fin.

Without any physical remains for direct examination, however, the Gambian creature cannot be positively identified one way or the other. But the Gambian find suggests, at least, that not all of the reptiles of prehistory died out with the dinosaurs.

Burnham himself says: 'When I think of the coelacanth I don't like to think what could be at the bottom of the sea. I'm not looking for a prehistoric animal, only trying to identify what was the strangest thing I'll ever see. I couldn't believe this creature was lying in front of me. Even now I can remember every minute detail of it. To see such a thing was awesome.'

ESCAPING DETECTION

The *magnum opus* of sea-monster studies is Belgian cryptozoologist Dr Bernard Heuvelmans's *In the Wake of the Sea Serpents*. In this, Heuvelmans analysed 587 sea-monster sightings made between 1639 and 1964. After disposing of hoaxes, misidentifications and reports too vague to be useful, he was still left with 358 sightings, and was able to sort these into nine basic types.

These are the 'long necked' sea serpent – the most often-reported of all sea monsters, with four flippers, a cigar-shaped body and a capacity for swimming very fast indeed – which grows to between 15 and 65 ft long; marine saurians, seen only in tropical waters in mid-ocean, which may reach 60 ft in length; merhorses; many-humped monsters; super-otters (not reported since 1848 and possibly now extinct); many-finned monsters; super-eels; fathers-of-all-the-turtles; and yellow-bellies. The last Heuvelmans believes may be an as yet unidentified fish, possibly a shark.

There is no logical reason why the seas should not be hiding any number of unidentified species of animal (especially if they are both shy and few in number) from the official catalogues of marine science. They will doubtless continue to roam the oceans, bemuse and astonish those few who are lucky enough to spot them, and be overlooked by the guardians of orthodoxy. Probably the creatures themselves would prefer it to stay that way.

Above: *The alleged sea monster photographed by Robert Le Serrec at Stonehaven Bay, Hook Island, Australia, on 12 December 1964.*

PAGAN PLACES, PAGAN POWERS

The ancient remains of powerful pagan civilizations cast long shadows into the present. The bright light of scientific investigation only deepens the mysteries surrounding the strange occurrences and unnerving experiences, and makes the shadows darker still...

While the Earth is full of strange, unexpected and inexplicable creatures, it is no less replete with mysterious and enigmatic works of mankind itself.

The ancient remains of lost civilizations – the great monuments of Stonehenge in England, Carnac in France, the Serpent Mound in Ohio, USA, the stone circles of West Africa – are only the most renowned of a myriad of such sites whose purpose is still obscure and whose meaning has been all but lost with the passing of those who built them.

Yet the world's mysterious places exercise a perennial fascination. They do so not simply because we still do not really understand them, or because they are awesome in themselves; but partly, at least, because we sense that they were enigmatic even to the people who created them.

Very strange things are traditionally said to happen at ancient sites. Very strange things still happen in such places today.

THE PETRIFIED MAIDENS

According to the pioneeering 'Earth mysteries' researcher Paul Devereux, a number of people have had bizarre

Above: 'Earth mysteries' researchers Paul Devereux (left) and Ian Thomson. Of all those attempting to unravel their mysteries, Paul Devereux has produced some of the most original and credible theories concerning the meaning and purpose of ancient sites.

Opposite and left: The Rollright Stones in Oxfordshire, which have been known to exert very peculiar influences on people in their vicinity.

MANY STONES RESIST ANY ATTEMPT TO MOVE THEM AND IF THEY ARE SHIFTED, WILL RETURN TO THEIR ORIGINAL RESTING PLACE.

The Pipers, in Cornwall (right), *are reputedly the petrified remains of the musicians who incited the Merry Maidens* (below) *into such a frenzy that they danced till they collapsed – and themselves turned to stone.*

experiences while passing along a particular 300 yd long stretch of a country lane that runs past the ancient stone circle called Rollright in Oxfordshire, England. One, a member of the Dragon Project research group, was watching a car containing two people approach the stone circle along the road – when the vehicle vanished. On another occasion, a scientist saw a huge, dog-like creature with coarse grey hair momentarily appear and then vanish. Another witness, a woman, saw an old-fashioned gypsy caravan briefly appear and then disappear in much the same way.

Odd occurrences have been associated with such megalithic sites since time immemorial, and the stones, then as now, have been held to possess mysterious powers. There is nothing new about stone circles attracting, or generating, spectres, visions of fairies and other odd creatures from folklore such as black dogs (an instance of which was, presumably, what was seen by the scientist noted above). At the Bryn-yr-Ellyllon mound near Mold in Wales, for example, a huge golden figure has been seen on many occasions – and the name of the barrow itself means 'hill of the goblins'.

It is commonly believed that the number of individual stones in certain circles cannot be counted, although many sites are associated with specific numbers, most often the key mystical figures of three, seven and nine. Possibly one reason they

cannot be counted is that, so the legends say, they can move of their own accord. Many stones are reputed to resist any attempt to move them but, if they are shifted out of place by some means, will put themselves back where they came from. Others are still more independent. One such is the Enstone near Oxford – it is particularly regular in its habits: it reputedly takes a drink every midnight at a neighbouring stream.

There may be a connection between this kind of belief and the tradition that many standing stones, especially groups of them,

Circular, holed stones like this one at Men-an-Tol, Cornwall (**left**), *are reputed to have mysterious powers of healing – as do the spring waters at Bath* (**below**). *Both sites are notable for a higher-than-usual amount of radioactivity, which some believe may have a homeopathic, healing effect.*

were once people, now petrified. The Merry Maidens in Cornwall are so called because that is what they once were – a mite too merry, perhaps, as they danced themselves to exhaustion and turned to stone where they collapsed. Nearby are the musicians presumably responsible for whipping them into their frenzy: the Two Pipers, and the Blind Fiddler, now pillars of granite. The Rollright Stones are reputedly a king and his knights, petrified by a witch.

Not all the powers associated with the ancient stones are so spooky: many have the reputation of being able to heal or impart healing properties. Water that has been splashed on the stones at Stonehenge will cure ailments. Sick children were traditionally passed through the hole in the famous Men-an-Tol in Cornwall. Other sites have the same capacity, especially those associated with water such as holy wells and ancient spas. There is evidence that the baths at Bath, for instance, have been regarded as curative for some 7000 years.

All these unexpected properties have one thing in common: they suggest that there is something strangely alive about these places. They are, in other words, places where a peculiar kind of energy concentrates. This half-hidden idea is reflected in another tradition about ancient places – that many of them are associated with dragons. Stories, myths and legends occur in virtually all cultures, all over the world, of a serpent, worm or dragon whose qualities are, to say the least, peculiarly ambiguous. So it is worth taking a brief

Serpents have always been seen as both threatening and promising, from the Garden of Eden (above) to St George's encounter on behalf of an endangered virgin (below). Dragons might be defeated by the most irreverent means (above right), but gaining the treasure or knowledge in their keeping would always bring fresh challenges.

survey of dragon-lore before pondering how it fits into the puzzle of the ancient sites.

THE DRAGON GUARDS

In the oldest Indian and Babylonian myths, which are roughly 4000 years old, the destruction of an enraged dragon brings the release of life-giving waters. These myths are not moral fables, but creation myths – poetic accounts of how the world was made. The importance of the dragon in these stories is that it releases an indispens-

able source of life and energy into the world – but at the price of having to confront the creature.

Everyone familiar with Genesis is aware of the double nature of the serpent in the Garden of Eden. It is an actual, physical presence, and also it represents a singular moral dilemma. To follow the path of the serpent, as Adam and Eve do, is to lose paradise and innocence but to gain knowledge and moral responsibility – free will.

This theme runs through all serpent myths, all over the world. In Anglo-Saxon Britain, the epic – and essentially pagan – poem *Beowulf* revolves in part around a fire-breathing 'worm' – in other words, a dragon – who is enraged because one of the aging Beowulf's subjects has stolen a cup from the hoard of treasure it has guarded for three centuries. (The poet makes a point of saying that dragons seek out and hoard treasure.) In killing the dragon, Beowulf is mortally wounded. Once again, the serpent is associated with something desirable and yet destructive. His power is also, finally, irresistible, and is potent in the cause of both good and ill.

Anglo-Saxon culture, like any other, had many roots. What we see in *Beowulf* is the fruit of tendrils that reach back to Norse and Celtic mythology, and beyond that to legends that have their known beginnings thousands of years ago, in the mythology of the Indo-European peoples of Central Asia. From the point of view of an investigation of prehistoric sites, what is also significant in this European dragon tradition is its connection with another piece of lore about the sites themselves: that is that many of them are reputed to be built on hoards of buried treasure.

The golden spectre seen at Bryn-yr-Ellyllon may be a reflection of this folk-memory. Like the stones themselves, some hoards have minds of their own. At the neolithic mound of Willy Howe in north-eastern England, there is a tale that local people once attempted to dig out the chest of gold concealed at its centre. They tried to drag it from the earth with horses, but the chest simply burrowed deeper into the ground. As might be expected, many such prehistoric hoards are said to be guarded by dragons.

TREACHEROUS ELEMENTS

It's clear that in Western and Middle Eastern dragon-lore, the creature has both a material and a spiritual energy, but it is one that is neither simple nor entirely trustworthy.

Take the paradox that these fiery creatures have an affinity for water, for example. Water is the most treacherous element as well as the most vital. The same may be said of fire, the other 'element' that is inseparable from any concept of dragons. One hidden lesson here seems to be that both the most basic materials of survival and the great abstractions like moral freedom have a potential for both good and evil. Another hidden message is that struggle is inherent in all our dealings with the contradictory forces of life, despite the fact that we depend on them – or perhaps *because* we depend on them.

The most fundamental lesson that underlies these perceptions is that these are eternal verities; they are the very basic stuff of life. And so the spirit of the dragon never entirely dies. Indeed, in the Babylonian myth, the dragon was also the mother of all living things and, despite being slain, continues her immortal

Above: *The Neolithic mound called Willy Howe, in Humberside, rumoured to hide a hoard of gold that physically resists any attempt to remove it.*

Below left: *The raw power of water – an element for which the fiery-breathed dragon, paradoxically, has a special affinity. In Babylonian myth, the dragon who is mother of all living things reveals herself in ferocious storms at sea.*

> **AS THEY ATTEMPTED TO DRAG THE TREASURE CHEST FROM THE GROUND, IT BURROWED DEEPER INTO THE EARTH.**

Above: *Chinese dragons control the weather – a realm as changeable and unpredictable as dragons themselves.*

WE ARE CONFRONTED WITH SOMETHING ABSOLUTELY FUNDAMENTAL IN THE HUMAN PSYCHE.

existence as a monstrous serpent who makes herself visible in wild storms at sea.

Dragons are everywhere associated with the most fundamental aspects of life. In the Mayan culture of central America, which flourished between about AD 150 and AD 900, the serpent was 'lord of fire and time', and was also responsible for causing floods, earthquakes and storms. It is strange, given the distance between the Americas and Asia, that Chinese dragons are so similar in this respect.

In China, a vast and intricate dragon-lore grew up that detailed not only how long a dragon might live (5000 years) and how many scales it had (81 or 117, depending on the school of thought) but the medicinal virtues of its teeth, liver or saliva and the significance of its behaviour as an augury of the weather.

Chinese dragons are, by Western standards, quite benevolent, but they too have an ambiguous nature. They are capable of shape-shifting, appearing in the guise of familiar animals at will, and, most importantly, they control the weather – which, as everyone knows, is neither predictable nor always benign. And to this day the Chinese believe that their dragons must be appeased and placated. The art of *feng shui*, which means 'wind and water', is entirely devoted to avoiding any disturbance to the 'paths of the dragon' (*lung mei*) when siting buildings in the landscape. Expert geomancers – 'earth diviners' – make elaborate calculations to ensure that this balance of nature is maintained. A famous modern example of their work is the alignment of the Hong Kong and Shanghai Bank in Hong Kong.

One of the most baffling and yet fascinating of all the enigmas associated with prehistoric sites and 'Earth mysteries' studies is the universal nature of dragon-lore. That the same image should reflect so many similar intuitions in so many different cultures, separated by huge gulfs of time and geography, suggests that we are confronted by something absolutely fundamental in the human psyche. And more: that this in turn suggests that the human mind has grasped something crucial about the nature of the Earth itself.

We have, in the dragon, an extraordinary concentration of ideas: a mythical beast that guards material or spiritual riches; the

energies of the elements; and a connection with sites of 'Earth energy'. Researchers have also established that there is a connection between the ancient sites, the so-called ley lines that often connect them, and UFO sightings. Is it possible that dragons and UFOs are different forms of the same 'Earth energy'? And if so, are they shaped by the mind into the form most suited to a particular epoch – or do they cause the mind to perceive them in the most acceptable way?

That there are energies in the Earth, that they are most powerful around prehistoric sites, and that they have real effects on human consciousness, is attested not only by the *feng shui* geomancers and the long traditions of folklore – but by modern reports too.

WEIRD SENSATIONS

Paul Devereux collected one such account from local government official Peter Thornborrow. He was walking through the stone circle called Long Meg and Her Daughters in Cumbria, when he was suddenly assailed by a bizarre sensation of dizziness. He felt, he said later, as if he was 'not really there…not really in the same time'. He leaned against one of the stones to recover his normal senses. It responded by giving him what he could only describe as 'an electric shock'.

Devereux has also recorded that in 1986, as a young couple were driving on a country lane beside Carn Ingli, a peak and sacred site in the Preseli Hills in Pembrokeshire, west Wales, the girl felt a weird sensation of physical discomfort. She was sure the feeling was caused by the peak. The pair decided to test the idea. They drove on until the girl felt normal again, and then turned the car around and drove back over the same route. Once again, as they neared Carn Ingli, the strange and uncomfortable sensation returned.

Modern experience and traditional lore thus combine to confirm the strangeness of prehistoric sites. There is a long-standing belief that experiences like the two recounted above and the legacy of folklore clinging to these ancient places indicate that some form of paranormal or psychic energy is at work in them. Since the turn of the century, psychics have attempted to

Left: *The ancient stone circle known as Long Meg and Her Daughters in Cumbria. Virtually all such sites were created with stones in places that show anomalies of magnetism, gravity, or radioactivity. This may account for the bizarre psychic experiences that some have reported having at Long Meg and other similar locations.*

Below: *Local co-ordinator for the long-standing Dragon Project research group Roy Cooper tests the Rollright Stones for radioactivity.*

pick up the local 'vibrations' at standing stones, circles, barrows and mounds, and since the 1930s dowsers too have tried to unravel the secrets of these places. Unfortunately, the claimed results and 'discoveries' at any one site have been as many and various as the number of psychics or dowsers who have tried their skills there.

The aptly named Dragon Project was launched in England in 1977 to bring a comprehensive set of research methods to bear on the question of what kinds of energies might be present at prehistoric sites. The project decided to pursue two parallel lines of investigation: there would be room for dowsers and psychics to follow their own form of detective work, while a variety of scientific detection instruments would be used to search out and record the more conventional physical attributes of the sites.

This has involved recording levels of magnetism, radioactivity, infra-red radiation, among known physical forces, as well as recording and studying unexplained but theoretically conventional effects such as the strange light phenomena that have long been reported at or near many ancient sites. The psychic side of the research has been as inconclusive as any of the other attempts to use mind power to probe the secrets of the ancients, but the second, scientific line of enquiry has thrown up some intriguing results. Although this kind of monitoring deals in the standard scientific measures of physics, the actual

levels discovered at the sites have been by no means conventional or consistent with normal, average ('background') levels for the areas concerned.

Science has begun to confirm folklore.

Right: *A kiva – an underground chamber used for ritual purposes – once used by the Anasazi people of Mesa Verde, Colorado.*

Below: *Possibly one of the world's holiest places – the Chalice Well at Glastonbury, whose waters are mildly radioactive.*

SECRET KNOWLEDGE – SECRET PURPOSES

At Long Meg, where Peter Thornborrow had the bizarre experience described earlier, Dragon Project researchers found that several of the standing stones there had small patches on them that were emitting a constant stream of gamma rays – in short, they were radioactive. The stones concerned were granite, which is naturally radioactive, but not to the degree of these particular stones. And it is distinctly unusual for granite to emit radiation of any kind from concentrated energy points such as these stones possessed.

This may or may not have been responsible for Thornborrow's experience, but researchers have noted that in places where natural radiation – from granite or other radioactive minerals, or from radon gas seeping from the ground – is higher than normal, some people have experienced apparently altered states of consciousness. Monitoring the radiation levels around the Rollright Stones revealed a fascinating fact about the 300 yd stretch of country lane where at least three people – whose accounts we gave above – had reported seeing spectral visions. Geiger counters showed far higher than normal background readings of radiation here.

Its source, the researchers concluded, was probably in energetic rocks in the hardcore used to lay the road's foundations. This, like the stones at the ancient site, had come from local quarries – which suggests that whoever put the Rollright Stones in place was aware that the local rock had very special qualities. Those qualities were

RADIOACTIVE BURIAL CHAMBERS

People have experienced different strange effects at other sites with greater than the usual 'background' natural radiation. At Boleigh Fogou, an Iron-Age underground stone chamber or 'souterrain' built from granite in Cornwall, a psychologist saw mysterious swirls and points of light moving over the inner rock surfaces. Similarly, inside the 5000-year-old Cornish dolmen called Chun Quoit, archeologist John Barnatt and photographer Brian Larkman both saw bands of light flashing along the underside of the capstone.

Most of Europe's ancient underground chambers of this kind are in areas whose basic rock formations are of granite, or where uranium has been found, so it can hardly be insignificant that in North America, Pueblo Indian underground ritual chambers, known as 'kivas', were likewise built in uranium-rich areas of what are now the Southwestern States. Bearing that in mind, it comes as no surprise to learn that the King's Chamber in Egypt's Great Pyramid was specially clad in granite, and that when members of the Dragon Project monitored the King's Chamber they found

interesting to them because they served their purposes. The key question after that is: what were their purposes?

Some other odd qualities of ancient sites may help to get us nearer the answer to this crucial question.

ONE OF THE HOLIEST PLACES IN THE WORLD IS SAID TO BE — RADIOACTIVE.

Left: *Stones at the top of the Akapana pyramid at Tiahuanaco, Bolivia, twist a compass needle out of kilter.*

Below: *Castlerigg stone circle near Keswick, Cumbria, where weird lights have been seen, and whose westernmost stone has unusual and powerful magnetic properties.*

Above: *Gors Fawr stone circle in Wales. Rough and desolate today, this was once a major ritual centre, like Stonehenge* **(opposite)**, *the most elaborately built of all the ancient megalithic sites.*

enhanced radiation levels there, at levels at least as high as those found inside the granite monuments of Britain.

The great stone sites of the ancient world are not unique among ancient monuments in registering unusually high – although by no means dangerous – levels of nuclear radiation. Holy wells, too, can be mildly radioactive, and there is evidence to suggest that at such 'homeopathic' levels nuclear radiation is actually beneficial, not harmful. As mentioned earlier, the famous hot springs at Bath, England have been known as healing waters for some 70 centuries, and are mildly radioactive. The waters of Chalice Well, Glastonbury – one of the holiest places in the world, if the legends are to be believed – are said to be radioactive. Dragon Project researchers have also recorded higher-than-average readings from geiger counters at a number of holy wells in the Celtic fringes of Britain in Wales, Cornwall and Scotland.

MAGNETIC MAGIC

Ancient sites, stone circles and solitary standing stones have all been known for decades to have strange effects on compasses and lodestones. Go to a standing stone or similar ancient site and the chances are it is in a place where there are peculiarities in the Earth's local magnetic field, or that it throws the standard measuring equipment – the gaussometer – out of true by a marked margin.

The Dragon Project found that scattered about Carn Ingli were areas where there were powerful anomalies in the local magnetic field. In these places, compass needles point south instead of north, and gaussometers show unexpected readings. As for individual stones creating bizarre magnetic effects – or being carefully placed where those effects are most marked – there is a host of instances. At Castlerigg, Cumbria, only the westernmost stone, alone among 38 stones at the circle, affects a compass needle. At the Gors Fawr stone circle in Wales, the outlying pillar, which indicates the direction of the midsummer sunrise, is also the only magnetic stone at the site. A serpentine outcrop on Mount Tamalpais, San Francisco (a magical place for the local American Indians), similarly causes compasses to spin. There are many other examples, and they can be found all over the world.

Still more strange is another magnetic anomaly that Dragon Project researchers have found at many ancient sites. They discovered that some standing stones show sudden fluctuations in their magnetic fields that last for only a few hours. Similar effects were found, quite independently of the Dragon Project work, at the Rollright Circle by the retired engineer Charles Brooker, who reported his discoveries in the international journal *New Scientist* in 1983.

The nature of these short-lived magnetic pulses is not understood by modern science, so what significance they may have had for the ancients so many thousands of years ago must be today entirely a matter for speculation. But then so is the means whereby the peoples of the ancient world, lacking modern instrumentation, recognized these qualities in the sites and in the stones they chose, in the first place. And *why* they chose them for these qualities is another question altogether.

THE STONES ARE SINGING

Some of the unexplained phenomena at ancient sites would not have needed any exotic instruments to detect. One is the often-reported appearance of peculiar and apparently intelligent lights in, around or near prehistoric remains. Another is the persistent presence of inexplicable noises at these places.

While alone inside Stonehenge one early morning in 1983, Gabriele Wilson heard a 'ringing' sound from one of the stones. At midsummer in 1987, Michael Woolf and Rachel Garcia heard 'a sudden, muffled thunderclap' that seemed to come 'from beneath the earth' at the 11 ft tall Blind Fiddler stone in Cornwall. Other researchers at the Rollright Stones have reported curious clicking noises issuing from the ground at night.

The ancients themselves witnessed such odd sounds at their sacred sites, as well. The two 60 ft tall statues known as the Colossi of Memnon, in the Valley of the Kings in Egypt, were cracked during an earthquake in 27 BC. After that, the northernmost of the two statues began to emit a strange sound at dawn each day. The noise was variously described as 'soft' and 'bell-like', 'a musical note' and even (by contrast) like 'a cord snapping'. People flocked from far and wide to the massive statue in the belief that it would act as an oracle. The sounds stopped when the cracks were eventually repaired.

Whatever the cause of these particular noises, modern researchers have long known that sounds at extremely high 'ultrasound' frequencies – well beyond the range of normal human hearing – can be detected at dawn coming from standing stones.

In January 1987 Dragon Project workers discovered that a 3 ft band around the middle of the tallest stone at the Rollright Circle was the source of a signal being picked up by their ultrasound receiver. The signal always ebbed away as the day wore on. It is possible that these signals were the by-product of transmissions from nearby military telecommunications stations, resonating in crystals in the stones. There is nothing secret or occult in the fact that crystals are sensitive to radio waves. On the other hand, the effect could be caused by some unknown process occurring in the Earth itself.

CENTRES OF POWER

The folklore interpretation of the weird sounds and lights that have been heard and seen around ancient sites has been quite

THE GREAT STONE STATUES BEGAN TO EMIT A STRANGE SOUND AT DAWN EACH DAY.

The Colossi of Memnon in Egypt, which gave out bizarre singing noises after they were cracked by an earthquake in 27 BC.

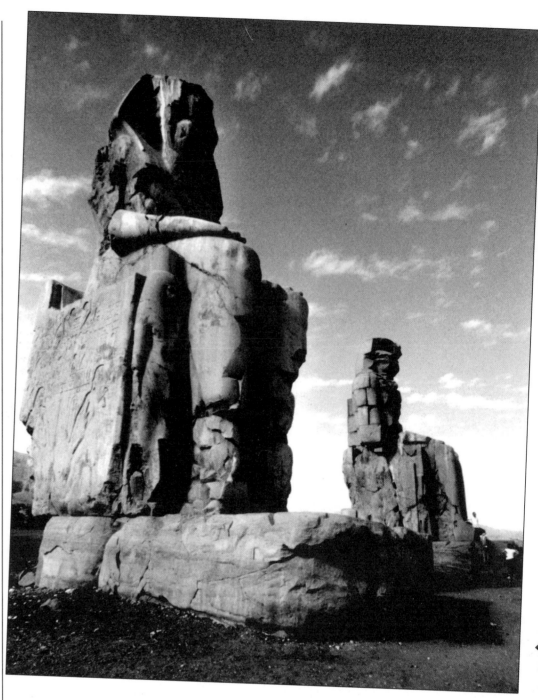

logical, but it has also probably been back-to-front.

People who have intuitively recognized something strange about the ancient places have attributed other signs of their uniqueness to the spirits, ghosts or even fairies to whom they feel these places belong. But almost certainly this view is the wrong way round. It is much more likely that the sites for stone circles, burial mounds, kivas and other ceremonial centres were chosen exactly because they were (in the eyes of the builders, those who saw them first) already magical. Throwing out strange noises and weird darting lights, such sites were advertising themselves as ideal for magical purposes.

As we have seen, these signs were also signals – that still stranger effects would take place in these places on the minds of those brave enough to enter them. How those effects were taken advantage of and controlled is one of the central mysteries of the purpose of the prehistoric sites.

This mystery may not be entirely unsolved, but even to glimpse the solution, we must first look at the stars, the Sun and the Moon, the tree at the centre of the world, and at mysterious patterns on a parched desert floor.

CELESTIAL SIGNS IN SACRED PLACES

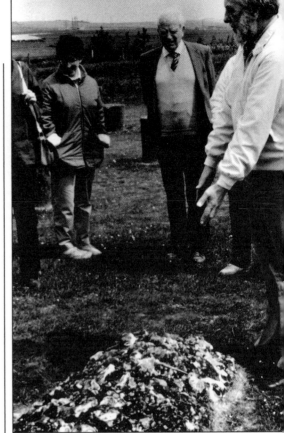

Right: *Professor Aubrey Burl* (at right), *an authority on Stonehenge, whose work has helped demolish the myth that the site was an astronomical 'observatory' rather than a temple.*

Stonehenge, with its toppled stones and sad grandeur, is but the last in a series of sacred temples which changed drastically in both appearance and purpose over several thousand years. The original Stonehenge was a place of earth and timber – and rotting corpses.

Stonehenge (previous page and below) *is perhaps the most impressive of all megalithic monuments – yet its architectural splendour hides the slow spiritual decay of those who built it.*

The curious physical qualities of the sites where the ancients built their sacred places must have had specific advantages for those who used them. But what did they use them for?

One tenacious myth that has taken hold in many a mind is that the prehistoric temples and stone circles were used as astronomical observatories. This idea has been going the rounds since the late 19th century, when archeologists first recognized the way that Stonehenge, on Salisbury Plain in England, was built to coincide with a number of seasonal astronomical events. It was full of 'sight-lines' between the stones to significant sunrises, sunsets, phases of the Moon, and movements of the stars.

Many of the conclusions drawn by the early pioneers of astro-archeology have since been found to be – not to put too fine a point on it – wildly wrong. In spite of this, their ideas were revived in the 1960s. It is in fact illogical and outmoded to believe that a place like Stonehenge could have been used to watch and mark the behaviour of the Sun and Moon and stars.

The illogic of such an idea is easily exposed, for to build these sites in the first place, someone must have known *beforehand* all the astronomical phenomena to which their stones are so precisely aligned. The builders of the great prehistoric monuments had already made their observations of the sky and taken their measurements on the ground long before they laid a single stone. It is an especially piquant notion that such a massive construction as Stonehenge could ever have had the flexibility that is essential to a real observatory. Such places are not evidence of some kind of primitive science, as the first researchers believed, and as many who mourn for the 1960s still do today.

'No astronomer-priests surveyed the skies there,' Professor Aubrey Burl has written plainly of Stonehenge. 'Superstition, not science, dominated the minds of its builders.'

COSMIC DRAMA

Not only did the ancients see the material world in a different way from us, they seem to have found a link between space and time, and between solid reality and the realm of the spirit. Ancient astronomy was a religious quest, and Stonehenge is one of the most dramatic and visible pieces of evidence of that. Its role was not that of being a record or marker of a scientific view of the Universe and the Earth within it. It was built as a stone stage set for a cosmic drama. But by the time it reached its most complex form in stone, it was not even the greatest of such constructions in the ancient world.

Stonehenge seems to be a symbol of enormous stability, and that it is a monument to an apprehension of cosmic reality that has long since been lost only makes the splendour of the place, emptied now of its original meaning, all the more moving. But the toppled stones and magnificent relics of grandeur that we see today are in reality the last and, amazingly, the least complicated of a series of temples that were built on this single site over a period of some 16 centuries.

A TEMPLE OF DEATH

The very first Stonehenge was made not of stone, but of earth. Around 3200 BC the skin-clad peasants of the farming tribes of Salisbury Plain dug out a wide circular earthwork known as a henge. It had an inner bank broken by what seemed to be two entrances. One was 35 ft wide on the north-east arc of the henge. The second was narrower, and was set precisely south

of the centre of the henge. The builders probably found this point by halving the distance between the points on the horizon where the midwinter Sun rose and set.

In 1723 the antiquarian William Stukeley (who also discovered the other great prehistoric site in southern England, Avebury) noticed that the south-west-to-north-east axis of this original construction, and thus the north-eastern 'entrance', was almost in line with the midsummer sunrise. Later researchers realized that Stukeley had made an error. The builders had been interested in another heavenly body: not the Sun, but the Moon.

Outside the north-east gap in the earthwork each year, they had set up a post in line with the most northerly rising-point of the Moon. Unlike the rising-point of the midsummer Sun, this moves gradually

Above: *The Moon, not the Sun, was the most important heavenly body to the builders of the first Stonehenge.*

Above: *The Heel Stone casts its shadow toward the circle at Stonehenge.*

THE FIRST STONEHENGE WAS A TEMPLE TO THE MOON, NOT THE SUN; AS SUCH IT WAS A TEMPLE OF DEATH.

---

across the horizon between two extremes, over a period of 18.61 years. The ancient builders had recorded this slow motion over six cycles and more than a century of observations, until they were certain of the most northerly point where the Moon rose. They aligned one side of the north-east 'entrance' with this point.

The first Stonehenge was a temple to the Moon. It was also a temple of death.

ROTTING CORPSES

For more than a millennium the ancestors of the first builders of Stonehenge had buried their dead in long barrows that pointed to the Moon somewhere between its midwinter rising-point in the north and

Example from Suffolk (**right**) *of an intricately patterned artefact of the Beaker Folk.*

its midsummer rising in the south. For these people, death and the Moon were inextricably bound up together.

The north-east 'entrance' was in fact a window, one side aligned to the midpoint of the Moon's arc, the other to its northernmost rising. Marking these lines of sight were pairs of tall stones at the edges of the causeway. On its eastern side the middle of the lunar cycle was marked by the now-fallen Slaughter Stone. The famous Heel Stone, beyond it, was never a pointer for the midsummer sunrise. It was always a lunar marker.

At the centre of the first Stonehenge was a 100 ft wide roofed building where corpses were laid until their flesh had rotted, and then the bones would be buried in the long barrows on the plain outside. This rite was long practised in Neolithic Britain and was always associated with the Moon.

The power of this strange holy mortuary was enhanced by more dead, deliberately acquired. In ditches at the ends of both entrances through the earthwork lie the bones of adults and children, sacrificed to the cold-faced, sky-sailing, shape-shifting silvery goddess of death that these people worshipped.

A TEMPLE OF THE SUN

Around 2200 BC, a new people arrived in the region and converted Stonehenge into a temple of the Sun. Whether they were a branch of what archeologists call Beaker Folk or not, their characteristic remains are bright-red, geometrically patterned beaker pots. Teams of men dragged Welsh blue-stones into the already ancient earthen enclosure and set them up in two concentric circles. Some of the slabs were shaped as lintels, imitating the earlier timber building.

The stones themselves had come from the Preseli mountains in south-west Wales. Legend said they were brought the 200 miles from those bleak, rainswept hills by none other than Merlin, the mysterious guardian mage of Camelot and King Arthur. Later, theories as elaborate as any concocted to account for the building of the pyramids in Egypt sprang fully formed from the brains of unwary academics to explain the logistics of moving the giant

Left: *Carn Meini in the Preseli Hills in Pembrokeshire. Bluestones from here were used in building Stonehenge, and how they made their way from west Wales to Salisbury Plain long remained a mystery.*

HUMAN SACRIFICES –
ADULTS AND CHILDREN –
WERE MADE TO THE SHAPE-
SHIFTING SILVERY GODDESS
OF DEATH.

---

blocks to Salisbury Plain in an age that lacked the wheel. The favourite theory had copper prospectors hauling the things on logs and floating them down rivers.

The real history of Stonehenge is full of surprises. The intrepid-stone-age-trucker theory is even less likely to be true than the rather more pleasing image of Merlin wafting the stones across the Severn with his wand. Archeologists have found a Welsh bluestone in a barrow that was abandoned 10 centuries before Stonehenge was built, yet only seven miles from the site. The prosaic truth is that the bluestones were literally lying about the local landscape, waiting to be used by anyone who was minded to do so. They were dumped there by glacial action, perhaps as long as 8000 years before Stonehenge was even thought of.

The people who brought the stones changed the axis of the henge. They widened the right-hand side of the north-east 'entrance', so that the middle of the break in the earthwork was now in line with the midsummer sunrise. On either side of the Heel Stone, they dug an avenue that led downhill towards the River Avon.

For these people, beakers and Sun-worship went together. Tissue-thin discs of gold have been found with the pots in their distinctive round barrows and are decorated with circles and crosses, and they seem to be symbols of the Sun.

The newcomers placed four stones at the corners of a large rectangle around the unfinished stone circles. Now called the Four Stations, these created three sightlines. The short side of the rectangle they made indicated the midsummer sunrise, while the long side pointed to the northern moonset. Down the line of one diagonal one saw – can still see – the point on the horizon where the Sun sets on May Day, later to be celebrated by the Celts as another Sun festival, Beltane, which means 'the shining one'.

Death was still the essential reason for the existence of the rearranged temple. The burials round about, in the new round barrows, continued apace, dug with sweat and toil from the chalky downland. And on the new axis of the henge, not far from the centre of the stone circles, the newcomers dug the grave of a man, and laid his bones

Below: *Representation of the death of Arthur. The Arthurian age is linked in legend with the stones that make up Stonehenge.*

Above: *A Bronze Age warrior. About 4000 years ago, Stonehenge was rebuilt for the last time to create the monument whose remains we know today* (**below right**).

THE SUNSET OF STONEHENGE

At the height of the Early Bronze Age, around 2000 BC, Stonehenge was remade yet again – into the form whose battered and crumbling remains we can see today. By then, great cemeteries of round barrows were crowded into the landscape around the temple. In them lay the bodies of chieftains and their women, clothed in finely woven wool, with their weapons, and household items made of bronze, copper, jet, amber, faience and gold. In a few centuries Stonehenge had changed from being a simple peasant mortuary chapel to a grand cathedral, the exclusive last resting-place of the rich, the powerful, the hard and the mighty.

One might speculate easily on how the new Stonehenge was pressured into being. Possibly the warrior chieftains had grumbled about the poor place the temple was, until their demands forced a monument befitting their status from a servile priesthood and a crushed people. Possibly the priests themselves had become the real powers behind these tiny thrones, and flaunted their power in this last grand architectural gesture. In any case, Stonehenge was rebuilt, but it was no longer a place for the common people. It became weighty and overwhelming, with room only for the priests, their acolytes, and the privileged.

The bluestones were torn out at the

in it with the head to the north-west, looking towards the midsummer Sun. His life gave life and strength – it consecrated – the magical place on the borderline between here and there, the present and the future.

roots. From the Marlborough Downs, 20 miles away, gangs of the faithful or coerced somehow found the energy to drag massive sandstone blocks to the site, where they were shaped and erected in the circle that everyone now knows as Stonehenge. Thirty uprights supported 30 lintels. These stones, bizarrely, were finished by using carpentry techniques – as if no one knew how to dress stone, and as if the builders could not tear themselves away from the memory that this site had once sported a timber building. Inside this forbiddingly atavistic ring of stones, in a monstrous horseshoe pattern, were set five trilithons, five separate, towering archways, each of two pillars topped by a lintel.

The axis of the henge was reversed yet again. The horseshoe of trilithons was open to the north-east but rose in height toward the tallest of them, to the south-west, where the Sun would be seen setting at midwinter – but only by the few for whom there was room in this spectacular but now cramped and darkened place. Astronomically, it was, quite literally, but a gigantic shadow of its former self. The only cosmic matter of interest to its priests was the single alignment to the midwinter sunset.

Whole epic novels might be written about how the mighty slowly but surely toppled after that. The process took 1000 years, and no doubt the last of them were

the most tragic, dramatic, bloody and meaningless. The system decayed; the great stones became empty at the heart. By 1000 BC Stonehenge had been deserted. The place was left to the shrieking crows, the wind, and the teeth of the rain – and to the curiosity of those who came nearly 30 centuries later, and wondered what the place had ever been for.

ANCIENT LIGHTS

The builders of the ancient sites did not create them all solely as places from which to peer out and watch the Sun and Moon performing in predictable order. The events and effects they designed them for may have been predictable, but they could be far more spectacular than a mere moonrise or a sunset. One of the ways the ancients celebrated their festival days was to create dramatic lighting effects within the very monuments themselves.

These ancient lightshows, as veteran earth mysteries researcher Paul Devereux has dubbed them, needed a dark stone interior for their full effect to be seen and felt, and, without exception, they were designed to form part of some kind of religious ritual. A good example of this mixture of exploiting astronomical observation and religious significance can still be seen at Burro Flats in the Simi

Below: *The passage-tomb at Newgrange, Ireland, in whose interior astonishing effects of sunlight and shadow are created at midwinter.*

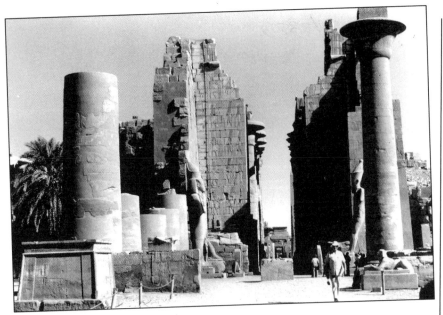

Above: *Karnak temple in Egypt, which is aligned to the midsummer sunset.*

Hills, near Los Angeles, California. Here, a panel of Chumash Indian rock paintings marks the site of a long-dead medicine man's shrine. The paintings are of centipede-like creatures, winged human forms, clawed animals, and handprints. These are traditional and ancient signs of sanctity in American Indian lore.

For most of the year, rock overhangs shelter the paintings at Burro Flats but, on midwinter's day, the rising Sun sends a shaft of light through a natural gap in the rocks that surround the shrine, pointing a pencil of light across the paintings. Thus the inner world of the Earth and of human art, spirit, the emotions, and the mind – and the outer world of the sky and its heavenly bodies were linked.

Nowhere is this link between the inner and the outer universe made more clearly or more spectacularly than at the complex of monuments in the Boyne Valley, Ireland. The best-known of these is the vast Newgrange mound, which is a huge construction penetrated by secret passages and chambers whose ultimate purpose can only be guessed at. Inside the mound, a passage 60 ft long leads to a high stone chamber at the heart of the mound. Here, the rising midwinter Sun sends its light through a roof-box built above the entrance to the passage. Only on midwinter's day can the beam of sunlight reach to the back of this central chamber.

On the Loughcrew Hills of Ireland, US artist Mark Brennan and his research colleagues found that at the equinox – the two days in the year when night and day are of equal duration – the rising Sun shines into a cairn there, and that it frames a rock carving at the back of the inner chamber. The carving was a Neolithic symbol for the Sun. The eight rays emanating from its centre represented the eight ancient divisions of the year.

The temple builders of Neolithic Europe used this kind of effect in many sacred mounds. The entrance passage of Maes Howe, Orkney, for instance, is aligned with the midwinter sunset. The passage forms part of an intricate web of alignments that cover the whole island.

Inside the 5000-year-old stone chamber of Gavrinis in northern France, a block of quartz stands exactly half-way along the length of the entrance passage. It can hardly be an accident that it was placed at a point where the beams from the sunrise, pouring down the passage at midwinter, would intersect those from the Moon at a key point in the 19-year lunar cycle. Archeologist Aubrey Burl suggests that the builders of Gavrinis used quartz in this place because it would glow dramatically white when the Sun and moonbeams played on it.

THE HEART OF THE EARTH

Similar effects were put to work at the temple of Karnak in Egypt. Much of the surviving temple complex dates from the New Kingdom (1567–1085 BC), but the place was regarded as sacred for centuries before that. Through all its long history, the major astronomical axis of the site remained the same. In the 1890s, the astronomer Sir Norman Lockyer calculated that this axis pointed towards the midsummer sunset. He pictured the dying rays of the Sun reaching in to illuminate the image of the god kept in the darkened sanctuary that lay on the axis deep within the temple.

In the southern hemisphere is the Torreon, in the Inca citadel of Machu Picchu, Peru. The north-eastern window of the inner sanctum of the temple was cut to receive the beams of the midwinter sunrise (which occurs on 21 June in the southern hemisphere). Beneath this inner window is an altar-like rock that has been carved so that a sharp cleft, at right angles to the window, divides it in half. When the Sun

Left and below: *The stepped pyramid at Chichen Itza, Mexico, comes alive at the equinoxes as light and shadow create a representation of Kukulcan, the feathered serpent to which it is dedicated.*

rises at midwinter, its light floods in through the window, falling parallel to the cleft. It is possible that originally a frame hung from the carved knobs that protrude from the otherwise featureless wall in the Torreon, supporting a plumb line that would have thrown its shadow along the cut edge on the altar stone at the same time as the slice of sunlight lit it up.

On a ledge near the top of the 430 ft high Fajada Butte in Chaco Canyon, New Mexico, three fallen slabs of rock allow sharp shafts of sunlight through onto the rock wall behind them. A thousand years ago the Anasazi Indians (who lived here and to whom the place was sacred) carved two spirals into the rock face so that these 'Sun daggers' would cast their shadows on them in distinctive patterns at the equinoxes and at midsummer and mid-winter.

Further west along Chaco Canyon is the ruin of the Anasazi's great kiva, Casa Rinconada. This 12 ft deep, 63 ft wide circular ceremonial structure was built so that it lay north–south, east–west, and like Stonehenge has an opening in its wall to the north-east. The rising midsummer Sun casts a beam of light through this aperture onto the opposite wall of the kiva, illuminating one of six irregularly spaced wall niches.

The ancient builders thus symbolized how the outer universe of Sun and Moon always penetrate to the heart of the Earth. But this truth, which is reminiscent of the black and white dots in the ancient Chinese yin/yang symbol, was a fact of life to these people, whose lives reflected the constant interaction of both. Earth and sky were but aspects of the same thing to them.

THE HITCHING POST OF THE SUN

As the Sun gives light, so it also casts shadows. This fact was not lost on the ancients in their ceremonies and in the way they built their sacred places.

In Mexico, the Indians used shadow in a particularly flamboyant fashion, and with perfect symbolism. The so-called Castillo at Chichen Itza on the Yucatan peninsula is a Toltec-Mayan stepped pyramid originally dedicated to Kukulcan, the Feathered Serpent god. A spectacular light-and-shadow picture forms on the Castillo at the spring and summer equinoxes. In the last hour before sunset, the stepped, north-west corner of the pyramid throws a serrated shadow onto the west-facing balustrade of

**THE SHADOW ATTACHES
ITSELF TO THE STONE
SERPENTS' HEADS AND
WRITHES DOWN THE HOLY
PYRAMID.**

**THE PAGAN PEOPLES
FEARED THE SUN MIGHT
DISAPPEAR FOR EVER AT
MIDWINTER.**

Below: *The entrance stone at Newgrange, Ireland. Its enigmatic markings, and those on the kerbstones* (opposite), *may represent the Sun – or may be a record of images seen by entranced priests. The stones all play a part in the 'sacred lightshow' that takes place at Newgrange at the midwinter sunrise.*

its northern staircase. This produces a pattern of sunlight and shadow that looks strikingly like the body markings of the rattlesnake common to the region. At the bottom of the balustrade are serpents' heads, carved in stone. To these the shadow attaches itself, completing the image of the sacred snake, writhing down the holy pyramid.

In the last refuge of the Incas, the mountain-peak citadel at Machu Picchu, Peru, the small but highly significant Intihuatana is carved from a granite outcrop that sits on a naturally pyramid-shaped spur. The Intihuatana is an upright pillar, no more than a foot high, projecting from a complex, asymmetrical platform made up of a variety of odd surfaces and projections.

The name Intihuatana means 'hitching post of the Sun', which is a sure indication that this strangely fashioned (or adapted) feature must have played a vital part in the major Inca festival of Inti Raymi. This took place every winter solstice – the shortest day of the year – to 'tie the Sun'. The ritual prevented the Sun from moving any further north in its daily round and stopped it being lost for ever.

SHADOWS OF THE SUN

At Ireland's Newgrange, the American artist Martin Brennan noted something else besides the entry of the midwinter sunbeam into the great mound. He found that the entrance stone and another 'kerbstone 52'

were part of the solar alignment of the site, and that some of the stones in the huge stone circle surrounding the mound also play a part in creating astonishing light-and-shadow effects on that crucial day of the year. And it was crucial: the prehistoric people of the Old World, like the Incas in Peru half a world away, also feared that the Sun might disappear for ever at midwinter.

At midwinter sunrise, as the roof-box at the entrance directs the Sun's rays deep into the mound, the shadow of one of the circle's stones points like a finger to the entrance stone and its vertical marking. At the same time, the shadow from a nearby stone strikes another carved kerbstone. With the complex interplay of shadow and light at the site, it is, as one commentator has said, 'almost as if the builders of Newgrange have left software running in their hardware'.

At nearby Knowth, another mound built like Newgrange with an inner passage and central chamber (and at about the same time, around 3700 BC), Brennan discovered that when the Sun sets at the equinoxes and sends its light down the entrance passage, a standing stone outside likewise throws its shadow onto the vertically grooved entrance stone.

At Castlerigg stone circle in Cumbria, England, photographer John Glover saw an extraordinary phenomenon during the midsummer sunset in 1976. Just as the Sun was sinking to the ridge on the horizon, Glover glanced behind him, and was amazed to see that the tallest stone of the circle was throwing a huge shadow right across the valley.

When the path of the shadow was surveyed later, the researchers found that the slope of the ground beyond the site was such that the shadow fell parallel to it and so extended far beyond the immediate ground. A conifer plantation stands in the way today, but originally it would have stretched for more than two miles across the moor.

THE LIGHT IN THE DARKNESS

Can we deduce anything from these alignments and angles, the subtle interplay of light and shade, or even from the final dark centuries of Stonehenge, with its fixation on midwinter and death, about the meaning of these astonishing constructions?

The answer is, tentatively at least, yes. As was remarked earlier, the symbolism of these ancient places indicates that for those who fashioned them with such care and attention, Earth and sky were not separate, but parts of a whole. There is more to be quarried here, however. Even the monumental morbidity of Stonehenge speaks of a fixation with wholeness – and by implication with *balance*, as if the ancients had anticipated and written in stone and ritual the words of Cranmer's prayerbook: 'In the midst of life we are in death…'

In the same way, the penetrating light of the Sun at sites all over the world is balanced by shadows; the dark created by light, the light known only in the darkness of a hidden chamber. Earth and cosmos were tied together by threads of light and a network of shadows in a kind of symbiosis. The one could not exist without the other, the ancients saw, and dramatized their intuition in their sacred architecture.

To them, Earth, Sun and Moon coexisted in a cosmic marriage. Part of the drama played out by the stones is conjugal: the long hard light of the Sun penetrating the secret passage of the Earth; the phallic shadow stretching itself and growing across the surface of the Earth's vast body. This was not a crass cartoon, a huge slide-show of sex and fertility, but an enactment of ultimate cosmic union.

And wherever this celebration of balance, of wholeness, of cosmic passion took place, the people could see that they were at the centre of the Universe, for here all things met as one. The ancient places were at the core of all existence.

> THIS WAS NO SLIDE-SHOW OF SEX AND FERTILITY, BUT THE ULTIMATE COSMIC UNION.

THE MYSTIC LANDSCAPE

For the ancients the Earth was a woman – a mother to be worshipped and cherished, and a lover to be erotically embraced. The secret places of her body were the most sacred sites of the pagan religions, but their true purpose remains mysterious...

A sense of centrality inspired the builders of the world's ancient monuments: they treated their creations as if they truly were at the centre of things, and placed them where the whole surrounding landscape reinforced and reflected that feeling. If need be they would mould whole landscapes to underline the importance of a particular site.

The image of the world's centre took a number of forms in the ancient world. One was the *omphalos*, the navel of the world. Another was the 'world egg'. Another was the 'world tree'. Derived from the Tree of Life were any number of more portable icons and symbols: particular, living, sacred trees, or so-called totem poles, or even a simple rod stuck in the Earth. Wherever these were, there – for the purpose at hand – was the centre of the world.

Marking that central point of the world was the first great magical act in creating sacred geography. Its spiritual importance is nowhere better illustrated than in the creation myth of the Zuni American Indians of New Mexico, who are probably descended from the Anasazi who built Chaco Canyon.

According to their myth, the first Zuni wandered for a long time, looking for a place of peace and stability, where they would settle. Frustrated in their search, they finally summoned *K'yan asdebi*, the water-skate, because his long legs could point in all the directions. A centre of a kind himself, he could surely identify the centre of the world.

This he did. He rose into the sky and stretched out his legs in the six great directions: the four cardinal points of the compass, and above and below. Gradually he came back to Earth, saying, 'Where my heart and navel rest, beneath them mark the spot and there build a town of the midmost, for there shall be the midmost place of the Earth-mother, even the navel...'

A VIEW OF THE GODS

The idea of the sacred centre is really an extension of the individual's perception that he or she already exists at the centre of his or her own world. Each of us looks out upon the world with an intuitive idea of six basic directions: front, back and sides, with the Earth beneath our feet, and the heavens above us. Wherever we are, we are always at the centre of our world.

At its deepest level, the meaning of a sacred site made itself felt through the action of the landscape on the mind, and the *reaction* of the mind to the landscape. Ultimate reality could not be apprehended

Above: *A Quechua boy. These Peruvian Indians still maintain an elaborate mythology of Earth and stars that places their settlement at the very middle of the Universe.*

Opposite: *The Athenian treasury at Delphi. This sacred site is a 'navel' of the world – the centre of the cosmos for those who worshipped there.*

THE SACRED CENTRE WAS
THE HOLIEST OF PLACES:
IT WAS THE PLACE WHERE
THE ACTIONS OF THE GODS
– AND SOMETIMES THE
GODS THEMSELVES –
COULD BE SEEN.

Below: *Sioux Indians in an ecstatic dance, with their medicine man or shaman in a buffalo hide. The centre of the cosmos for the Sioux is Mount Harney, and the shaman's staff is also a symbol of the 'world axis' around which Heaven and Earth revolve.*

without this exchange between mind and landscape. The place represented a whole that fused together three things: time – made visible as a result of the astronomical alignments of the place, and its play of light and shadow; space, in the form of the landscape that reflected the work of the gods; and man-made imagery, the sign of human consciousness and awareness.

The sacred centre was sacred exactly because it was the place from which the movements of the Sun and Moon were observed and measured against the skyline, and because it was the place from which the actions of the gods – sometimes, even their very shapes – could be witnessed. It was the centre because all things were joined there.

THE ORACLE OF DELPHI

The best-known omphalos in the Old World is the temple complex, sanctuary and ancient home of the oracle at Delphi, Greece. According to Greek myth, Delphi was founded after the chief of the gods, Zeus, sent out two eagles from the far ends of the Earth; where their flights crossed would be the centre of the world. The eagles met over Mount Parnassos, on whose southern slopes Delphi was built.

Reflecting this legend, some classic depictions of omphalos stones (which existed at numerous sacred sites in ancient Greece) show two birds perched on them, facing in opposite directions. Two such stones survive at Delphi today. One is in the complex of temple ruins and is a cone of grey stone shot through with quartz veins. The other is now in Delphi's museum. It is egg-shaped, about 3 ft high, and covered by a delicate interlaced pattern carved in bas-relief.

THE STOREHOUSE OF THE DEAD

The Andean Indians have a very different concept of the stars in the sky than the Western notion of a series of constellations like a picture-book of mythical beings. To the Quechua Indian community of Misminay, who live near the Vilcanota River, about 30 miles north-west of Cuzco, Peru, the Milky Way is the key feature of the night sky.

They call the Milky Way *Mayu*, 'River'. They see it as the heavenly version of their River Vilcanota, which flows from south-east to north-west, and in Quechua myth is said to dump its waters off the edge of the Earth into the encircling void of the heavens. These waters are collected in the north-west by the Milky Way which carries them through the sky before letting them fall to Earth and rise again in the east. As the waters are carried overhead, some of the moisture drops to Earth again as rain. The terrestrial and celestial rivers fertilize land and sky.

From Misminay (as from any fixed point on the Earth), the Milky Way appears to swing across the sky, so that every 12 hours its southern and northern ends respectively appear to rise from the south-east and north-east. In a 24-hour period, this apparent movement draws two lines across the sky that intersect directly overhead. The Quechua call this zenith point *Cruz Calvario*, the 'cross of Calvary', borrowing the term from Christian missionaries, whose work among them was not entirely successful.

This division of space by the Milky Way is reflected on the ground in the layout of the Misminay settlement itself. Two footpaths and irrigation canals running side by side form an X-shaped cross on the ground. Their intersection is called *Crucero*, 'the cross'. This corresponds to the 'crossing point' of the Milky Way in the sky overhead – Calvario.

Crucero is the place in Misminay from where the horizons of the 'four quarters' of the world are marked by the local people. Each direction is meaningful in Quechua mythology, and the meaning of each is reflected in house groupings in the village and in the significance the people give to certain sacred peaks beyond. The north-west–north-east quarter, for example, is associated with the ancestors, and the holy mountain on the horizon in that direction is called *Apu Wanumarka*, the 'Storehouse of the Dead'. Here again we have a linking of Earth and sky, life and death, past and future, the interpenetration of space and time in which each part gains its meaning and nourishes the spirit only because it is part of the whole image of the Universe that the people entertain.

THE GOLDEN NAVEL OF THE EARTH

Most ancient peoples possessed some concept of the sacred centre, and it could take many forms. It could be stone, as at Delphi or Delos in Greece, a holy city like the Incas' Cuzco (the name means 'navel' in the Quechua tongue), or a rock, as it is for the Semangs of the Malay Peninsula, where *Batu-Ribn* emerges at the centre of the world. It is a rock, too, at Jerusalem, that great centre sacred to Judaism, Christianity and Islam alike, and it is a rock too in Mecca.

The world centre could also be a peak, a 'world mountain'. To the Sioux Indians of the American Great Plains, the centre of the world was on Mount Harney. Israel may boast *three* world centres including Jerusalem – Mount Tabor, whose name may mean 'navel', according to the historian Mircea Eliade, and Mount

Above: Mount Fujiyama, Japan's sacred mountain whose volcanic nature makes it a prime symbol of the raw power hidden within the Earth.

Above: *Priests of the Japanese Shinto religion, which is the world's oldest and is based on a celebration of the mysteries of the Earth.*

THE TREE OF LIFE IS A SYMBOL OF WHOLENESS AND SPIRITUAL STABILITY, BUT AT ITS ROOTS GNAW THE CORRUPTIONS OF MODERN CIVILIZATION.

Gerizim, which, Eliade maintains, was 'undoubtedly invested with the prestige of the centre, for it is called "navel of the earth"'. Buddhists too have their world centre in Mount Kailash in Tibet, the legendary 'Mount Meru', centre of the cosmos to believers. People still make pilgrimages to the remote mountain, to make a ritual tour around it. Some even make the circuit on their knees. In Japan, the volcanic cone of Mount Fujiyama is sacred; the Shinto religion centres on living earth mysteries.

The notion of the holy peak is deeply embedded in the human psyche. Croagh Padric in the west of Ireland, sacred to the great Christian saint of the island, is likewise a centre of pilgrimages and rituals, which are possibly not Christian at all in origin but an adaptation of a far older tradition.

Besides appearing in stones, rocks and mountains, the centre of the world might be represented by a pole, or even a pit dug in the ground. The 'world tree', in particular, was a universal form of the sacred centre. The world tree connected the heavens and the underworld, but was also the axis from which the middle world, the Earth, oriented itself. It was the 'still point of the turning world', but also a kind of conducting rod between the upper and lower parts of the whole cosmos.

The Yakut tribes of Siberia believe that at the 'golden navel of the Earth' stands a tree with eight branches. In Norse and Old German mythology, the world tree was named Yggdrasil, and trees that symbolize the sacred centre live on in traditions as diverse and distant from one another as those of the Australian aborigines and American Indians.

Like the sacred mountain, the roots of the world tree reach into the human mind, and the sap still rises in this ancient image. It is found in (relatively) modern opera, in Wagner's reworking of the German myths in *The Ring*, and even in English literature.

The German composer Richard Wagner (right) *and the English novelist D.H. Lawrence* (far right) *both used the ancient symbol of the World Tree in their work.*

Left: *The Paps of Anu in County Kerry, Ireland – the bare breasts of the Earth Goddess Anu, who is still regarded with awe today.*

THE LANDSCAPE RESEMBLED A WOMAN WITH HIGH BREASTS, AN ARCHED STOMACH AND LONG LEGS WITH THE KNEES DRAWN UP.

Below: *Scholar Paul Devereux, whose studies have contributed vastly to understanding the use and meaning of the ancient world's sacred sites.*

In *Women In Love*, written in the 1920s, D.H. Lawrence was still conjuring with the tree of life as a symbol of growth, wholeness and spiritual stability, at whose roots gnaw the corruptions of modern 'civilization'.

A SLEEPING BEAUTY

Gazing out from their cosmic centre across the landscape, the ancients saw a very different world from the one we think we are looking at. Agriculture, where it existed, was neither a cosy calling pursued by a romanticized minority nor a business, but a battle with nature that involved most of the tribe most of the time. Nor were the deserts dead but photogenic places. The whole of the landscape was alive.

Since Earth and the heavens enacted a cosmic marriage, it is not surprising that many ancient peoples around the world saw in the hills and moors, deserts and mountains around them the shape of a vast goddess, the Earth Mother. She did not *give* life to the land; she *was* its life, and they saw her in it.

The island of Jura off the west coast of Scotland has a range of mountains called the Paps: the central peaks are symmetrical and rounded like breasts. At Ballochroy, on the Kintyre peninsula on the mainland, the central stone of three menhirs has a smoothed side that faces the most northerly of the Paps, Beinn Corra, 19 miles distant across the sound. Behind this peak the Sun sets at midsummer.

On Lewis, the most north-westerly of the major Hebrides islands, the Pairc Hills are known locally as the 'Sleeping Beauty': they resemble the profile of a woman lying on her back. From the cluster of stone circles and settings known as the Stones of Callanish, it seems that when the Moon rises at its most southerly point during its 19-year cycle, it comes forth from the Pairc Hills. At this one time in the cycle it is as if the Sleeping Beauty gives birth to the Moon.

Two symmetrical, rounded hills near Killarney, Ireland, are known as the Paps of Anu. In the Irish myths, Anu is the mother of the last generation of gods to rule the Earth, the legendary Tuatha de Danaan. According to Celtic scholar Dr Anne Ross, these hills are still regarded with awe today. They 'personify the powers of the goddess embedded in the land', and Anu 'is still regarded as the local fairy queen'.

From the Greek island of Poros, off the north-east coast of the Peloponnisos, the mountains on the mainland are seen by local people as outlining the form of a woman lying on her back. 'The resemblance is indeed persuasive,' says the American historian Vincent Scully almost primly in *The Earth, the Temple and the Gods*, although he notes with some relish the shapes of 'the head low on the north, a long neck, high breasts, arched stomach, long legs with the knees drawn up'.

UPLIFTED BREASTS

In *Symbolic Landscapes*, earth mysteries scholar Paul Devereux draws attention to the vast number of Bronze Age Cretan figurines that exist of a goddess with her

Right: *Part of a ley discovered in Gwent, Wales, by Alfred Watkins, a pioneer in the study of enigmatic alignments in the landscape. The track in the foreground leads directly to Llanthony Priory, and continues (unlike any conventional path) in a straight line up the hillside.*

arms raised in a characteristic and apparently curious gesture. The best-known example is the faience Snake Goddess found at Knossos, the heart of the ancient Minoan empire on Crete. Both the figure's upraised arms and its breasts, emphasized by an open bodice, create a cleft shape that is a direct echo of the sacred landscape of the island. The courtyard of the palace at Knossos opens to the distant, cleft-peaked Mount Yiouktas. The palace's *propylaia* or entrance is precisely aligned with the mountain.

The Minoan bull ritual, in which young men and women seized the horns of a charging bull and were propelled over its back, also echoed the horned peak of Mount Yiouktas. We know about the ritual because it is detailed in frescos found at Knossos, and it was performed under the eye of the horned mountain.

'The landscape and temples together form [an] architectural whole,' Vincent Scully wrote of the ancient Greeks' perception of their surroundings. He believed that the Greeks had 'developed an eye' for 'specific combinations of landscape features as expressive of particular holiness'.

This perception of the interchangeability of land and spirit was not confined to Knossos by any means. Other Cretan palaces were built in a deliberate relationship with horned mountains.

Among them are Mallia, which points toward Mount Dikte, and Phaistos, which is aligned to Mount Ida. At Gournia, the palace faces two hills that Scully described as 'so close and rounded that a more proper analogy would seem to be more directly to the female body itself and they do closely resemble the uplifted breasts' of the goddess. He remarked too that the enclosed landscape around Gournia gave the 'inescapable impression' that the palace was being embraced in the arms of the Earth Mother.

Similarly, the characteristic gesture in representations of the goddess is found throughout the Mediterranean. The small terracotta goddess figurines of Mycenae on the Greek mainland have the same raised arms. Tombs in the Castelluccio cemetery in Sicily were carved to show a powerful figure with upraised arms, breasts and head. Pieces of pottery of the same period from Sicily, the Lipari Islands and southern Italy all have horn-like handles to create an image of a goddess with raised arms.

The motif is thousands of years old. Female figurines and pottery decorations from pre-dynastic Egypt, for instance, feature this sacred gesture of upraised arms. The psychologist Erich Neumann has suggested that this universally repeated gesture of the Earth Mother indicates prayer, invocation or a magical conjuring of the deity. What he might have added is

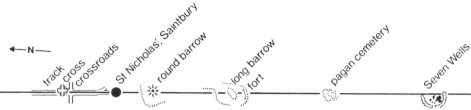

track | cross | crossroads | St Nicholas' Saintbury | round barrow | long barrow | fort | pagan cemetery | Seven Wells

the reflection that it also reinforces the impression that the ancients saw their world as a cosmic union in which spiritual energy is constantly cycling through the whole of creation.

For it can hardly be insignificant that the goddess is always portrayed as herself in an attitude of worship. The Earth Mother was not separate from the rest of the Universe, complacently receiving its supplications, but herself takes part in a mutual – and mutually invigorating – reverence. Time and space, people, gods, spiritual energy, Earth, Sun, Moon and landscape were all aspects of one another. The world was whole, and holy.

HOLY LINES

Of all the conundrums posed by the ancient world's mystical landscapes, the most baffling is the fact that most are built on, or in, straight lines of one kind or another. This puzzling feature takes many different forms around the world. Every one of them brings us back to one of the most familiar, yet most fundamental, of the 'Earth mysteries': the riddle of 'ley lines'.

The usual story is that leys were discovered by Alfred Watkins one sunny June afternoon in 1921. As the 66-year-old businessman was sitting in his car, gazing out over his native Herefordshire from Blackwardine, he glanced down at the map in front of him. It was then, in a sudden epiphany, that he realized that the pre-historic mounds, earthworks and standing stones of the country before him were arrayed in arrow-straight lines across the landscape.

Watkins was not, in fact, the first to notice this. Numerous researchers had recorded their findings prior to Watkins's 'discovery' of 1921. As early as 1846, for instance, the antiquarian Edward Duke had proposed that Stonehenge and Avebury, some 20 miles apart, were part of an invisible straight line across the countryside that passed through another stone circle and two prehistoric earthworks. Other scholars throughout the 19th century noticed similar alignments, and in 1904, Hilaire Belloc published *The Old Road*, in which he described medieval pilgrimage routes linking old churches in England and, drawing on his observations while travelling in the USA, the straight tracks of American Indians.

Watkins, however, provided a compre-hensive account for the ancient lines on the land. He believed they were the remaining signs of prehistoric traders' trackways, and they were straight because they had been laid out by line-of-sight. Watkins kept finding distinctive boulders on the lines he explored. He was convinced these were part of the original, prehistoric survey, and consequently called them 'markstones'. He also found old churches and crosses on the alignments which, he argued, were pagan – i.e. prehistoric – sacred places that had been commandeered by Christianity.

Watkins called his alignments 'leys' because he noted the word recurring in placenames on the lines. It comes from the Welsh word *llan*, which originally meant 'sacred enclosure'. The possible signifi-cance of this passed Watkins by, possessed as he was, like any good Victorian

Left and above: *The Saint-bury ley in Gloucestershire runs for about 3.5 miles through the Cotswold hills. The photograph shows a section near St Nicholas's church, facing south.*

> **ALONG THE INVISIBLE LEY LINES CHRISTIAN CHURCHES AND CROSSES HAD BEEN BUILT IN AN ATTEMPT TO DESTROY THE POWER OF THE SACRED PAGAN PLACES.**

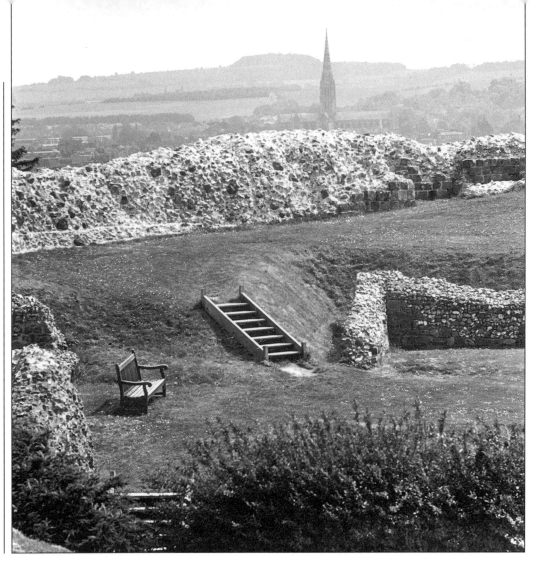

Right and below: *The Old Sarum ley in Wiltshire. The photograph shows the ruin of Old Sarum with Salisbury Cathedral in the distance.*

merchant, with the idea that the leys must have been trade routes. But the point was not lost on his contemporaries, the German researchers Josef Heinsch, who noted lines linking hills and old churches, and Wilhelm Teudt, who called the German alignments he discovered *heilige Linien*, 'holy lines'.

MYSTERIOUS ROADS TO NOWHERE

As Hilaire Belloc had realized, mysterious straight lines running through the landscape between ancient sites, and utterly regardless of their practicability as paths as they shot up sheer inclines and blithely disappeared over precipices, were not an exclusively European phenomenon. And as research and surveying and archeological digs continued, it became apparent that nowhere are there such enigmatic lines in the landscape as in the Americas.

The American Indians of antiquity made what are literally old straight tracks – they too ignored practicality for the sake of a ruler-like precision – and equally straight lines of sacred sites, shrines, holy rocks and wells. The remains of this curious practice can be seen all over the Americas, and it obsessed many diverse and distant American Indian cultures. One of the most intriguing of all these prehistoric straight-line systems is in the American Southwest: the 'Chaco roads'.

These are centred on Chaco Canyon, in the high mesa country of north-west New Mexico. They were made by the Anasazi, whose name is actually a Navajo Indian term meaning 'the enemies of our ancestors'. The Anasazi thrived in the Four Quarters area of New Mexico from about AD 800 to about 1300; some of them, in these latter years, clashed with the Navajo as they migrated into the region from AD 1000. The Anasazi developed a distinctive style of flat-roofed buildings made of mud, rock and wood, called pueblos.

Chaco Canyon was the prime Anasazi ceremonial centre. Here, the culture reached its height. Over the years, the pueblos grew into multi-storeyed terraced complexes now known as 'Great Houses', with walls, courtyards, and 'Great Kivas' – very large ceremonial chambers. There are nine Great Houses within Chaco Canyon itself, all built between AD 900 and 1115. The largest was Pueblo Bonito, covering some three acres.

CARVED THROUGH LIVING ROCK

The Anasazis' mysterious roads radiate in straight lines for many miles around Chaco Canyon. They are fully engineered, a fairly constant 30 ft wide, with spur roads about half as wide. At their borders are earthen ridges, lines of stones or drystone walls. Their surfaces were laid with compacted earth – or cut straight into the bedrock. The true extent of the Chaco roads became apparent only in the 1970s, when aerial photography revealed how vast the network was. With ground surveys and digs, archeologists have now mapped some 400 miles of these enigmatic highways.

Like similar sacred 'routes' elsewhere, the Anasazi roads are no respecters of difficult terrain if it stands in their way. When they reached the canyon walls, the Anasazi engineers carved staircases up to 25 ft wide from the living rock, straight down the canyon sides.

The Chaco roads throw up a host of questions. Why did a people with neither horses nor the wheel need these elaborate highways? Are they roads as such at all? Recent computer-enhanced infra-red aerial pictures taken by NASA only deepen the mystery. These have revealed the existence of rows of sections running parallel to the roads. What were they for?

There is a consensus among archeologists and scholars that the roads were ceremonial or sacred ways that linked the Great Houses, which seem to have been

Above: *An Anasazi Indian settlement huddles under a cliff face at Canyon de Chelly, Arizona. The whole of this bare and seemingly hostile landscape was sacred to this vanished people.*

Right: *The 'Cliff Palace', the largest of the Anasazi settlements perched high within the escarpment at Mesa Verde in southern Colorado.*

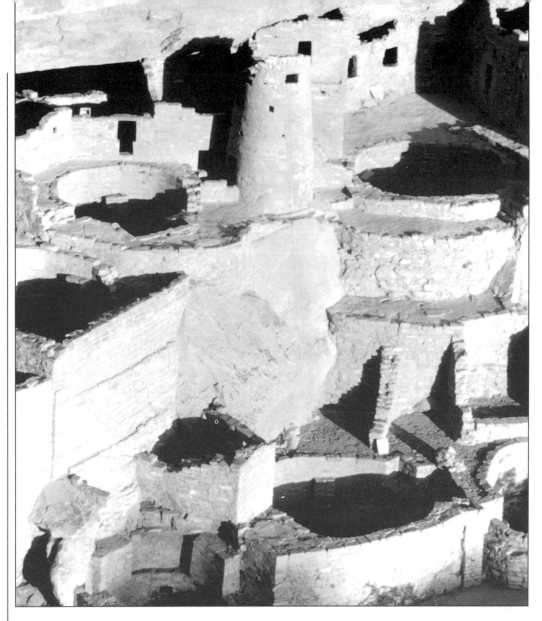

THE DESERT WAS LIKE A VAST DRAWING-BOARD COVERED WITH PRECISE AND MYSTERIOUS PICTURES — PICTURES THAT COULD BE SEEN ONLY FROM THE AIR.

ritual centres. Fragments of pottery have been found in limited areas along some of the roads, notably near Great Houses. Breaking pottery vessels has been an act of consecration in numerous societies in widely distant places all over the world. It was often associated with the dead. It is possible that the Anasazi considered the roads themselves to be holy. It remains – officially at least – a mystery as to who used them, and why they were so broad and so finely made.

INVISIBLE HIGHWAYS

Virtually every sacred site in the prehistoric world was linked with others, major or minor, by a radiating network of straight lines. Few were as elaborate or as easily detected in their heyday as the Anasazis' strange highways. Most were invisible, like the leys of Europe – which makes them, in a way, all the more mysterious. In rare cases like the Ohio effigy mounds and the vast drawing-board that covered the desert floor at Nazca, Peru, entire sites were devoted to creating miles of straight lines and, still more bewildering, very precise pictures that could be appreciated only from the air.

In cultures that enjoyed such a comprehensive world-view, and that had such a magical sense of the continuous life rolling through the whole of creation – which today we sterilize and alienate by calling it the 'environment' – the lines, visible or invisible, had to have meaning. Where do they fit in the weft and warp of this most tightly woven of all mythologies?

This has been the greatest enigma of all in the study of the ancient sacred places. It was also, as a handful of researchers have now realized, the biggest clue of all to the meaning and use of the prehistoric sites, and it was staring them in the face all the time.

A MAP FOR THE MIND

Previous page: *Parallel lines drawn on the desert floor at Nazca, Peru, disappear mysteriously into the distance. Straight lines like these, some miles long, are found on the Earth at ancient sites all over the world. Why were they so important to those who made them?*

AT ANCIENT SITES THE HERE AND NOW HAD LINKS WITH THE SPIRIT WORLD.

Below: *Michael Persinger, whose research suggests that ancient sites have qualities that enhance psychic perceptions.*

Fault lines, strange lights, magnetic and gravitational abnormalities – how do all of these fit together in the world's mysterious places?

So far, we have gathered up various enigmatic bits of information about the world's mysterious ancient places. They were most often built on fault lines, and these are places where strange lights and magnetic and gravitational anomalies abound. We've seen that these places can have bizarre *psychic* effects on people. Research by Professor Michael Persinger of Laurentian University in Ontario has even suggested that individuals become especially receptive to extra-sensory perception in the presence of the phenomena that cling to the ancient sites.

We know too that these places were seen by the people who built them as *cosmic centres* on which the Sun and Moon were deliberately focused. Most probably, the cosmic light shows were arranged to reinforce the sense of *universal* centrality of the shrine – its place between the Otherworlds. At the sites, too, the here and now was strangely interfused with the spirit world – whether in the form of the Earth Goddess or through the link between Heaven, Earth and Underworld that was symbolized by the 'world tree' or some other equally potent image. Many sites are associated with the dead. Finally, we have seen that these perplexing places are linked, or infested, by straight lines both visible and invisible.

How, or where, do all these aspects fit together? What is the missing link? A brief tour around one of the most problematic of these baffling monuments may let slip a few more clues.

DESIGNS IN THE DESERT

Probably the most famous of American Indian straight lines are the markings on the desert pampas around Nazca, Peru.

The Nazca lines were drawn by removing the desert surface to reveal the lighter soil beneath. The lines can be anything from a few dozen yards to several miles long, and pass straight over ridges. Interspersed among the hundreds of straight lines are a variety of line drawings, made in the same way, of animals, sundry geometric forms and irregular and regular abstract shapes.

It is easier to say what the lines and drawings at Nazca are not than to summarize what they might be. That they are not and never did form a landing-strip for 'ancient astronauts' is a statement scarcely worth making: the idea was never worth ten seconds of anyone's time. Nor are the lines aligned to the heavens in any more conventional archeo-astronomical sense. Work in the 1980s co-ordinated by Anthony F. Aveni of Colgate University, New York State, confirmed the finding by Gerald Hawkins of the Smithsonian Institution in the 1960s that none of the lines had any significant astronomical function.

Aveni and his colleagues did find that there is some pattern to the apparently random layout of the lines on the ground. Nazca's resident researcher Maria Reiche had noted what she called 'star-like centres', from which lines radiated like

Above: *The complexity of the lines and patterns at Nazca becomes clear when they are seen from the air. But why?*

rays from a sun. Aveni's team identified over 60 of these centres. They are set on natural hills or mounds, and at least one line from each centre connects it with another.

At these 'star-like' centres are deposits of small stones, shells and broken pottery fragments: signs of some kind of offering to the dead, as were found along the 'roads' in Chaco Canyon. In the 1920s, an elder of the Navajo Indians made the cryptic remark to archeologist Neil Judd that although the Chaco lines looked like roads, they 'were not roads'. The Nazca lines are not tracks, although they look like tracks. They start nowhere and end anywhere.

And the most impenetrable fact of all about Nazca is the line drawings. Why spend energy, which could barely be spared from the hard business of survival, on making pictures that no one could see?

Or *could* someone see them? And if so – how could they?

PATHWAYS FOR THE SPIRITS

Now let us go back to the straight lines. These are traditionally significant in other contexts. Here is another clue to the hidden meaning of the lines on the Earth – and of the ancient places themselves. There is a very ancient tradition that spirits – good and bad – move in straight lines. There is a huge global lore concerning the usefulness of knots in defending oneself against evil spirits, for instance. But straight lines can be used to encourage the intervention of the most beneficial spirits – most interestingly, in many widespread traditions, by using threads to provide a path for them.

Among some Australian Aboriginal tribes, a healer would treat a sick person by running a spider thread from the head of the 'patient' to a nearby bush. This, said the healer, was where the sufferer's spirit had fled from the ailing body. The filament provided a path for the spirit to return, making the patient whole again and banishing the illness.

Similarly, when dealing with sickness, the shaman (colloquially known as the tribal 'witch doctor' or 'medicine man') of the Buryat peoples of Siberia would place an arrow on the ground beside the patient's head and lay a red thread in a straight line, out through the entrance of the sick

> **STRAIGHT LINES ARE BY TRADITION THE WAY TAKEN BY THE SPIRITS – AND A THREAD COULD ENCOURAGE THEM.**

Above: *Seen at close quarters, the lines at Nazca seem almost insignificant. Yet enormous energy and devotion went into their design and maintenance. But how did their makers get to see the full effect of their work?*

SHAMANISM PERHAPS CAME TO THE AMERICAS ACROSS THE BERING STRAITS MORE THAN 15,000 YEARS AGO. IT REMAINED STRONG AMONG THE INDIAN TRIBES UNTIL RECENT TIMES.

person's tent, to a birch pole that he had previously stuck in the ground outside. The pole stood for the world tree, the link between this world and the realms of spirit, while the thread gave the sick person's soul a route along which to return to the body. The principle is almost identical to that of the Australian tradition.

Among the Maoris of New Zealand, the stem of a plant could be taken as a spirit 'line'. The *tohunga* ('healer') put the stem on a sick person's head and called on the evil spirit that was causing the illness to leave by the 'road' offered by the stem of the plant.

In terms of straight lines, the spirit world and ancient places, the most provocative of all these traditions of healing belongs to the Kalahari !Kung people. When they hold a trance dance, which involves hours of rhythmic movement and continuous chanting in the hypnotic presence of a fire, it's not uncommon for people to leave their bodies – to have what we would call an out-of-the-body experience. The !Kung call this state *kia*. Once in it, they can climb 'threads' up to 'where God is'. When they are with God, they can become healers. The !Kung say that then they are able to gaze into people's bodies with X-ray vision to see where any disease has taken root, and can then pull it out.

Here is a very clear indication that straight lines, contact with the spirit world *and* a state of trance are all closely related.

THE THREE WORLDS SYSTEM

The key that unlocks the mystery connecting straight lines and the sacred sites lies in the central fact about the ancient places themselves. That is: they were, exactly and literally, *central* to existence. The sacred centre was not only a place from which to make and take earthly bearings. It linked the 'middle world' of the here and now with the worlds above – Heaven – and below – the Underworld. The realms above and below were kingdoms of the spirit. Anthropologists call this cosmology the 'three worlds system'. It seems to have originated, possibly hundreds of thousands of years ago, with a form of religion known as shamanism.

When and where shamanism began is anyone's guess, but it probably arrived in the Americas with the peoples who migrated across the old land bridge over the Bering Straits somewhere between 15,000 and 25,000 years ago. The shamanic tradition remained strong and healthy among the American Indian tribes until very recent times because the Americas did not suffer the same cultural changes over the centuries as Eurasia did.

What is a shaman? The term itself comes from *saman*, the word the Tungus peoples of Siberia had for the 'elected member' of the tribe who could journey to the spirit worlds seeking healing for tribal members, finding lost or confused souls or seeking help for those in this world by divining the future or peering into the

Above: *Maoris performing invocation. Traditional Maori healing rites embody the concept of spirits using straight lines as pathways.*

Left: *A yarn picture made by the Huichol Indians of central Mexico. In the upper left of the picture are shamans, directing the life force of the Sun's rays as they fall on a cornfield. Note in particular what appear to be wings growing from the shamans' bodies – an indication of their capacity for magical flight in the realm of spirit.*

The Biblical image of Jacob's ladder (above) *as a connection between the spiritual realm and earthly life is echoed in shamanic traditions throughout the world. Like many shamans, too, Jacob had his visionary dream while sleeping on a sacred rock.*

THE SHAMAN'S CHANT,
OFTEN OF EERIE BEAUTY,
DISTRACTS THE LISTENER
AND IS BOTH HAIR-RAISING
AND HYPNOTIC.

remote past. The shaman was the intermediary between the tribe and the Otherworld of spirit, and he went to the Otherworld through an out-of-the-body experience. To his conscious self, this experience seemed to be the equivalent of flight above the Earth.

We can infer that this experience of flying was universal from many pieces of evidence. To begin with, shamans all around the world use strikingly similar metaphors to describe their journeys to the Otherworld. They say their spirits rise on smoke, ride along a rainbow, follow a flight of arrows, travel up a sunbeam – and so on. A particularly common image they use is the ladder, stretching from Earth to Heaven – just as Jacob's does in the Bible. He, significantly, also slept on a sacred stone.

ROUTES TO A TRANCE

The shaman used – and still uses – a variety of techniques to achieve the trance state. Among them were prolonged dancing, fasting and chanting. This last, incidentally, was not ordinary chanting. A large choir of Russian Orthodox monks sounds like a tin whistle with the croup in comparison to a shaman in full voice, and

the greatest cantor in Brooklyn might as well be a mosquito.

There are few sounds in the world more *un*earthly than the vocal performance of a Siberian shaman as he prepares to leave the mundane world. Bizarre but distinct whistlings come down from his sinuses and out of his nose and mouth, while he uses an astonishing, fundamental muscular control to produce a grim, low, rhythmic roaring from the diaphragm. On top of these various abnormal noises and mesmeric drones, he manages to produce a conventional human chant, often of eerie beauty, to distract the astounded listener. It comes as something of a surprise to discover that this last, most recognizable, sound is not actually coming out of his ears. The whole effect is both hair-raising and hypnotic, as well as inhuman – as it is surely meant to be, for him as much as for his audience.

Shamans may use other ritual tools at the same time or separately to induce trance. They include exposure to extremes of heat or cold, and a range of more or less horrifying methods of inducing pain and, hence, sensory deprivation. Shamans may also use hallucinogenic plants, foods or smoking mixtures (the 'peace-pipe' had a number of applications, but the ultimate effect was usually very peaceful, not to say positively dreamy).

The hallucinogens that the shamans used are interesting because many of these drugs gave their user a strong impression of flying. One 19th-century explorer into the South American interior described how he felt himself going on 'an aerial journey' as a result of drinking *ayahuasaca*, a potent Indian tincture made from a hallucinogenic vine. Modern dope slang reflects something of the same experience: among other things, one gets 'high', goes on a 'trip' and gets 'spaced out'.

The mental imagery induced by drug use and trance became central to many tribes' art. Among the rock paintings in a Chumash Indian shrine at Burro Flats, near Los Angeles, California, there is a series of geometric forms – dots, lines, crosses, circles and concentric rings. Similar patterns are found in rock art all over the world, and can be seen carved into the rock at many megalithic sites in Britain.

The source of these patterns is the human brain. The Tukano Indians of Colombia in South America (who use trance-inducing drugs in religious ceremonies) employ similar imagery as a basis for the decorative work on their pottery and clothing, and freely admit that these are based on the colourful but geometric forms they see under the influence of the drugs. The San (Bushmen) of the Kalahari, too, make no secret of the fact that the patterns and motifs in their own rock paintings are based on what their shamans see when in trance. These patterns were probably the original inspiration for another enigmatic pattern found at endless numbers of sacred sites all over the world: the labyrinth or maze.

Most significantly, the shaman moved from normal awareness to the Otherworld to the endless beating of a magic drum, which was covered in signs and symbols to protect him on his 'journey' elsewhere. He called his drum his 'steed' or 'canoe' on or in which he would travel to the spirit realm. One of the more intriguing discoveries

LABYRINTH AND MAZE PATTERNS FOUND AT ENDLESS NUMBERS OF SACRED SITES ARE PROBABLY INSPIRED BY FORMS SEEN UNDER THE INFLUENCE OF DRUGS.

Below: *A Siberian shaman's drum. His trance partly induced by its rhythmic reverberations, the shaman believed that the drum became a steed or canoe on which he rode to the Otherworld.*

PICTURES AND MOUNDS ON THE GROUND – WERE THEY TO BE SEEN BY THE MIND'S EYE OR THE SOUL WHEN OUTSIDE THE BODY?

Below: *The ceremonial costume of a Siberian shaman, dating from about 1890.*

made about these drums is that they produce sounds at extremely low frequencies – as few as four cycles per second. These affect the so-called *theta* brain waves, which are somehow involved in the deeper levels of dreaming, trance and meditation.

In the Siberian tribes, the shell of the shaman's drum was, in theory, made from a branch of the world tree (usually, in fact, a birch). Because of this magical link and through his hypnotic drumming, the shaman is 'magically projected into the vicinity of the Tree', as the anthropologist Mircea Eliade put it. In the tribes of central and northern Asia, the shaman would actually climb a birch tree during his trance, to show his spectators that he was indeed ascending the axis of the world and passing into the realm of spirit.

BIRD-MEN THROUGH THE AGES

Once up the tree, he flew. In some tribes, he waved his arms like a bird's wings when he got to the top. During his trance, the Yakut shaman of north-east Siberia also made dance movements and gestures to imitate the flight of a bird.

The image of flight was the unmistakable sign of a shaman in the ancient world, and is still in those cultures that have remained prehistoric and pre-industrial in spirit. The most frequent is the form of a bird perched on a stick (standing for the world axis or tree). From this token, the almost unimaginable antiquity of the shaman tradition becomes evident, for among the Cro-Magnon cave paintings of Lascaux, France, there is one of a bird-stick next to a man in a bird mask, who is apparently in trance. The painting may be a quarter of a million years old.

The Mississippian people, who flourished between about AD 900 to 1500, left many examples of pottery decorated with human–bird figures. Siberian shamans wore bird-claw shoes, and the Hopewell Indian shaman would decorate his robes with bird-claw shapes cut out of mica. In China, Taoist monks were called 'feather scholars', which reveals their original role. In Ireland, the Celtic Druids were believed to be able to take wing through applied magic. While North American shamans most often identified with the eagle, the ancient Indian text *Upanishads* calls the out-of-the-body spirit or soul 'the lone wild gander'; and the image flies from the tropics to the Arctic Circle, for geese figure prominently in Eskimo accounts of magical flight.

COSMIC CROSSING POINTS

The spirits, as we've seen in the accounts of healing techniques, for example, move in straight lines. Thus, the lines on the landscape and the straight flight of the shaman's spirit are almost certainly versions of one and the same thing. Whether the lines on the landscape ('They look like roads, but they are not roads') were put there to guide and protect the travelling spirit – a kind of safety net for the soul – or were put there to celebrate and consecrate shamanic flight, or were a *record* of these journeys in spirit, we shall probably never know.

But these various threads running through magical and religious lore, and the various clues at the ancient sites themselves, all point to the conclusion that the sacred centres were *shamanic* centres, with the life of the Universe – the Earth Goddess, the Sun, the Moon – focused upon them and throwing into relief their significance as crossing points between this world and that of spirit. And it seems clear that the lines radiating from them or linking them were highways of the soul in its out-of-the-body flight. The lines may well have been intended also as markers and guides for the spirits of the dead. The association between death and the ancient places is too strong, and the cultures that built them were too comprehensive in their symbolism, for there to be no connection.

The other mysterious aspects of the sites now fall into place. The pictures on the ground at Nazca, and the effigy mounds in Ohio, were made to be seen during an out-of-the-body experience. Again, we shall probably never know for sure whether they were seen purely in the mind's eye of the entranced and drugged voyager, or if his soul did literally wing its way along the leys and spirit paths laid out on the ground.

The geological abnormalities of the ancient centres too begin to make sense. Not only did the 'earthlight' effects around them, created by the anomalies in the Earth, proclaim them as unusual, but the enhanced magnetism or radioactivity of the stones in turn catalysed the trance of the initiated. Paul Devereux, who pioneered this interpretation of the ancient sites, speculates in *Earth Memory*:

'We can perhaps envisage the megalithic shaman, in an altered state of consciousness, lying or sleeping in head-contact with the stone of power at a site. This might have helped to engender special visions… in the way that [the Welsh holy man] St Byrnach…used the magnetically anom-

alous Carn Ingli to "speak with the angels".'

MAGIC JOURNEYS AND MODERN TIMES

In Europe and much of Asia, the early tribal societies that built the ancient sites developed into more complex forms. Shamans became priests, and the priests became kings. But they did not lose all their old associations with the old shamanic world.

The connection between the straight lines of spirit and the holy office of

Above: *A Taoist abbot, or 'feather scholar' – so-called because of the holy man's reputed ability to fly, an echo of shamanic origins.*

A STRAIGHT WAY CONTINUES TO SYMBOLIZE THE SPECIAL POWER ASSOCIATED WITH RULERSHIP, AND RECALLS SHAMANIC LINES.

Above: *A witch flies above the rooftops. The image is a buried folk-memory of the days when Scandinavian female shamans were said to be able to fly, and were pictured riding the sky on broomsticks.*

kingship can still be seen in a word like 'ruler' in English, which means both a straight-edge and a political chief. The word derives from an ancient Indo-European word, *reg*, which means 'movement in a straight line'. From the same root we also get the Latin *rex* (king) and thence the English 'regal'.

Look about the land, and one will see other relics of shamanic lines in regal institutions. Royalty has always surrounded itself with architecture that bristles with ceremonial ways, boundaries, royal routes and imperial avenues. Even the ceremonial ways of kingless Washington DC are laid out in straight lines. In London, the Mall is the broad way leading to and from Buckingham Palace. A sense that a straight way symbolizes a special power associated with rulership has thus survived.

Buried in the folklore of modern Western societies are other relics of the shaman's magic journey. The cosy image of Father Christmas flying in his reindeer-drawn sleigh through the magic midwinter night is a jolly version of the flight in spirit of Arctic European and Siberian shamans. The tribes there were reindeer herders. Their minds grew wings with the aid of the hallucinogenic fly agaric fungus – whose distinctive red and white cap is the colour of Santa Claus's robes. It may be significant too that Santa Claus lives at the North Pole – the axis of the world.

Another relic of the shaman's magical flight is the witch flying on her broomstick. Medieval witches took 'flying ointments' or 'witches' salves', which were made from hallucinogenic herbs that also created the sensation of flight by generating an out-of-the-body experience. The broomstick is an echo of the world tree; it also recalls the habit (still practised in the Americas) of sweeping clean the spirit paths on the ground to make the space sacred. The archetypal image of the witch may come from a Scandinavian sect of women shamans who practised a form of prophecy, known as *seidhr*, while in trance. They wore feathered garments to indicate their ability to fly when in this altered state of consciousness. They, too, were often pictured flying on broomsticks.

As a final provocative footnote to this labyrinthine tale, there is a strong hint in the Norse mythology that it was actually women who first taught men to 'fly'.

The world is a stranger place than it seems – an *even* stranger place than it *already* seems.